JUST SHY *of* Serenity

Just Shy of Serenity
Copyright © 2023 Nathan Lyle Cunningham. All rights reserved.

All rights reserved. No part of this publication may be reproduced, stored in a retrieval system, or transmitted in any way by any means – electronic, mechanical, photocopy, recording, or otherwise – without the prior permissions of the copyright holder, except by reviewer who may quote brief passages in a review to be printed in magazine newspaper or by radio / TV announcement, as provided by USA copyright law. The author and the publisher will not be held responsible for any errors within the manuscript. All characters appearing in this work are fictitious. Any resemblance to real persons, living or dead, is purely coincidental. Unless otherwise indicated, all scripture quotations are taken from the King James Version of the Bible.

FIRST EDITION
Published in 2023

Author: Nathan Lyle Cunningham
www.YouTube.com/NathanLyleOfficial
www.Twitter.com/NathanLyle

ISBN: 978-1-7343061-6-3

Library of Congress in Publication Data

Category: Relationships, Coming of Age, True Love, Mindfulness

Library of Congress Cataloging-in-Publication Data

Publishing Consultant & Designer: Eli Blyden | EliTheBookGuy.com

Printed & Published in the United States of America

Arthur's Note

Salutations valued reader. My name is Nathan Lyle Cunningham. If you've never heard of me, feel free to check out my autobiography *Everything is Impossible*. Did I just try to sell you a book in the introduction to a different book? Indeed I did. I'm broke right now and need as much money as you're willing to give me.

If you've never met me, know absolutely nothing about me, I imagine this introduction might be somewhat off-putting. Then again, if you have met me it might be even more off-putting. I'm talking too much. This book isn't about me. I already wrote that book. It's called *Everything is Impossible*. Oops. Did it twice. Sorry. I promise I'll stop.

There are two main reasons why I wrote this introduction. The first is to give you a preview of what you'll be in for should you choose to proceed beyond these pages. For you see dear reader, I shall be your narrator through this journey. Why not a fictional narrator you ask? Is it because I'm lazy?

Truth is, it was not my desire for this book to be an academic essay. Narratives such as this one are not meant to be studied in a classroom. They're best told when shared with friends sitting around a campfire. Passed down from parent to child as a cautionary tale of how not to live your life. That's why I didn't write this book. I told a story to my imaginary friends then sat down and typed every word I said.

Do me a favor? Please don't read this book. Don't just look at the words…witness them. Absorb them into your heart as if your grandfather was sitting across from you in the living room, relaxing in his favorite recliner, regaling you with tales of his youth. If it helps to imagine that Morgan Freeman is your grandfather feel free to do so.

Secondly, this is not a story of love. This is a story of pain. This is a story of acceptance. Learning to appreciate life for what it is instead of always lamenting what it isn't. I didn't write this story hoping to change the world or inspire anybody. I'm just a guy trying to work through some emotional baggage.

Table of Contents

Arthur's Note iii

CHAPTER 1
Kindergarten 1

CHAPTER 2
4th Grade 9

CHAPTER 3
6th Grade 19

CHAPTER 4
7th Grade 41

CHAPTER 5
9th Grade 59

CHAPTER 6
10th Grade 75

CHAPTER 7
December 14th 85

CHAPTER 8
11th Grade 99

CHAPTER 9
12th Grade 121

CHAPTER 10
College 149

CHAPTER 11
Two Years Later 189

Other Books by Nathan Lyle Cunningham...................... 205

JUST SHY of Serenity

BY NATHAN LYLE CUNNINGHAM

Just Shy of Serenity

Chapter 1

Kindergarten

The story begins as summer was ending. It was 1996 in San Antonio, Texas. A few weeks earlier a young woman moved into a small apartment with her son. She was an African-American woman, just under five and a half feet tall with a light complexion. A little chubby, but what American isn't. Straight black hair that stopped just above her shoulders.

Her son, Gerald, had recently turned four years old. Fairly dark skin, quite tall for his age, scrawny as a twig. His mom would cut his hair every two weeks. He wished she wouldn't. If his hair was longer it would hide his big ears and the kids at daycare wouldn't call him Dumbo.

From my perspective, it sometimes feels like modern parents hear the words "spare the rod and spoil the child" as an order rather than a warning. Gerald's mom was not a modern parent. If it seemed like Gerald was even thinking of considering the possibility of talking back she would not hesitate to smack him across the face. She loved bragging about how well-behaved her child was.

On the first day of kindergarten Gerald's mother made him a peanut butter and jelly sandwich. He told her he'd prefer bologna and cheese. She responded with the back of her hand.

"Don't be such an ungrateful brat. You lucky I make you food at all. Some kids are out there starvin' to death. Thank the lord you got such a carin' mother."

Gerald was the type of kid who would always hide behind his mother anytime a stranger tried to talk to him. Kindergarten was his first foray into the world of socialization. He failed miserably. He made it nearly the entire day without saying a word to anyone. Not even the teacher. He only opened his mouth to put food inside. He ate lunch sitting alone in the corner. During recess he sat against a wall reading a book.

A few days later, nothing had changed. His first week of school was almost over and Gerald had not made a connection with any of his fellow students. Then came that fateful Thursday. While most of the children were scattered around the room playing with Barbie dolls, Lego bricks and hot wheels, Gerald was sitting alone at a table coloring a picture of a zebra.

Gerald's process was simple. He closed his eyes, picked up a random crayon, chose one random object to use that color on, then set the crayon aside. The result was a purple zebra, a brown sun, a green sky, a blue tree with grey leaves, yellow grass and an orange lake. As he marveled at his masterpiece he heard a voice behind him.

"That's wrong."

Gerald turned his head to see Anjelica Ramos, a slightly chubby, light skinned Latina with long, thin black hair flowing down her back. She stood there clutching a teddy bear with a red bow. Her jaw hung open, revealing a mouth that was missing nearly half its teeth.

"The zebra's supposed to be black and white. Not black and purple. The sun is supposed to be yellow. The sky and water should both be blue. The grass and leaves are supposed to be green."

Gerald turned back to his picture.

"I know."

Anjelica tilted her head.

"If you know why'd you do it wrong?"

"Because if I did it right my picture would look as boring as everyone else's."

Despite what I'm going to tell you later in the story, Gerald did not fall in love that day. A stranger talked to him. He responded. In that moment no one would've guessed how important she would be to his life. If you already know...why'd you read ahead? You ruined the surprise.

For most of that year Anjelica was the only one who talked to Gerald. Were they friends? Not really. Every now and then she'd feel bad for the boy sitting alone and try to start a conversation with him. He never gave much effort to the conversation but he didn't chase her away either.

One day they were discussing the things they wanted most in life. Gerald only had one answer: the PlayStation. Anjelica's greatest fantasy was to live in the ocean. Ever since watching The Little Mermaid she's wanted to swim around under the sea like Ariel.

Kindergarten came and went with very little fanfare. First grade was much the same...with one tiny exception. A girl in class was throwing a birthday party. She wasn't planning to invite Gerald. Why should she? He's the weirdo who went out of his way to avoid interacting with anyone. The only reason Gerald received an invitation is because the girl's mother said it wouldn't be fair to exclude only him.

When Gerald first saw the invitation he had no interest in attending. Anjelica convinced him it would be fun. On her persuasion he decided to make an appearance. Had Anjelica known that her friend was planning to pull a mean prank she might not have been so insistent.

The specifics don't matter. You don't need to know whether Gerald had a bucket of paint poured over him, or fell into a huge pile of horse shit. What matters is that he was utterly humiliated and ran straight home to cry in the shower.

Anjelica did nothing wrong. She didn't help her friend set up the prank. She wasn't laughing along with the other kids. She didn't spend the rest of the school year teasing him like the rest of her classmates. She did nothing wrong. She did nothing. She said nothing. Just sat back and watched it all unfold in front of her.

Two years would pass before Anjelica heard Gerald's voice again. The summer before second grade Anjelica not only got braces, she got a big round pair of glasses. Either of those things could lead to ridicule. Both of them together automatically made Anjelica a pariah.

Gerald felt bad. Seeing Anjelica in pain hurt him more than he expected. On the other hand, it took all the pressure off him. Made second grade a lot easier than the first. In the middle of third grade a classmate threw a birthday party. As is tradition he invited every single kid in the class whether he wanted to or not. That's the only reason Gerald and Anjelica were there.

Not counting siblings and adult chaperones the majority of party attendants were between the ages of eight and ten. You know, that age when a boy starts to realize that girls smell nice but still uses cooties as an excuse to stay away from them.

It was a typical party with games and chocolate cake. Music was playing, no one was dancing. Of course, no elementary school party is complete without an overly optimistic busybody parent who doesn't understand the dynamic of interactions between children of this age. They put on a slow song thinking it'll be a cute picture. Then the boys and girls spend the entire song pressed against walls on opposite sides of the room.

The first verse passed and all the kids still had their eyes glued to the floor. Gerald was the first to raise his head. He scanned the opposite wall until he located Anjelica. As if sensing his gaze she lifted her head. They locked eyes. He smiled at her. She smiled back.

The song wound down and all the tension in the room began to dissipate. Then the busy body parent, instead of realizing it was the immaturity of the party guest that led to the outcome, incorrectly guessed that it was a poor song choice and put on a different slow jam. Half the kids in the room groaned and rolled their eyes.

As their eyes remained locked Gerald felt his heart racing. Some indescribable urge compelled him to move. Before he had a chance to talk himself out of it Gerald was on his feet headed for the other side of the room.

It was the most nerve-wracking experience of his young life. He was getting lightheaded and his feet grew heavier with every step. Anjelica was curled up in a ball that seemed to be gradually shrinking with every step he took toward her. Eventually, after what felt like and hour's walk, Gerald found himself standing in front of Anjelica wiping his sweaty palms on his pants.

"Hey."

"Hey."

"You uh…you wanna dance?"

Anjelica's first instinct was to say "no thanks" and send Gerald away. She was embarrassed to even be asked. She looked down the line and every girl on the wall was staring at her with wide eyes, eagerly anticipating her answer. She looked across the room and saw all the boys staring as well.

Her final decision was made when she looked up at Gerald. He had a gentle smile on his face but she could see the fear in his eyes. He looked even more nervous than she felt. It was very brave of him to walk over there and ask. So she took a deep breath.

"I'd love to."

Anjelica held out her hands. Gerald grabbed them and lifted her up. They walked to the center of the dance floor where they awkwardly fumbled their hands around for a few seconds before securing a comfortable placement. They didn't necessarily dance per se. They looked more like a pendulum, anxiously swaying side to side.

"I'm sorry."

Anjelica nervously squeezed Gerald's hand, worried that he wouldn't accept her apology.

"It's ok. I'm not very good at this either."

"No. I mean, the party. I'm sorry for what happened."

"What party?"

"In first grade. I'm sorry about what happened."

"Oh, that. It was years ago. I don't even think about it."

"That's good to hear. I'm still sorry though. And I swear I had nothing to do with it."

"I know."

"You're not mad anymore?"

"I never was."

"Then why weren't you talking to me?"

"I was embarrassed."

"You were embarrassed for two years?"

"You didn't talk to me either. I thought…I thought maybe you didn't like me anymore."

"Of course I like you. I just…I was scared. I'm sorry."

"You don't have to apologize. I don't need it."

"But you deserve it. How can I make it up to you?"

"By being my friend again."

"I was always your friend. I always will be."

They were so wrapped up in each other they didn't even notice the song stopped playing. They stayed there, holding each other, swaying back and forth as onlookers gawked.

I wish I could end the story here. Tell you they lived the rest of their lives happily together. Unfortunately, real life will never be that simple. They have many more struggles to endure before their journey ends. After all, this is only chapter one.

Chapter 2
4th Grade

Puberty. A necessary step on the journey to adulthood. A step most people would gladly skip if they had the option. The dreaded educational video that informs us of all the changes are bodies are about to go through. Being handed a stick that looks like chalk while they explain that you'll soon step out of the shower still smelling like dirty socks.

For Anjelica, turning ten was a huge deal. Her braces were removed. Her mom allowed her to start wearing contacts. She suddenly grew taller, now standing a few inches above everyone in her class. Worst of all, her boobs started growing. She didn't wake up one morning with and e-cup but they were certainly large enough that everyone in her class noticed.

The boys were mean, the girls were cruel. Through this period of constant change one thing remained the same… Gerald stood by Anjelica's side. They spent most of their afternoons and weekends together at her place. They read books, played games, danced to the radio. Gerald was the only one who never treated her differently.

Little did she know, every time they were in the same room Gerald's eyes would hardly move away from her chest. Whenever her eyes were aimed directly at him Gerald managed to meet her gaze. The moment her head turned his pupils dropped. He couldn't help it. Some evil force far stronger than gravity kept pulling his eyes down.

One afternoon they were doing homework in her living room when she asked him what answer he got for the fifth question. He was so locked on her chest that he didn't notice her head turning. She saw his eyes glued to her bosom, his jaw agape, with the tiniest drop of drool hanging from the corner.

"You pervert!"

Anjelica jumped to her feet. Gerald raised his head just in time to see her open palm headed straight for his face. As he rubbed his swollen cheek he looked up with shock. He saw the tears in her eyes and all he felt was guilt.

"I thought you were my friend but all this time you were just waiting for the chance to feel me up!"

"No. No, that's not…I just…I…"

"Get out!"

"I'm sorry."

"Get! Out!"

Gerald hurriedly shoved his books and loose papers into his backpack and rushed out the door. Anjelica ran up to her room and cried. From that moment on Anjelica refused to say a word to Gerald. It seemed like their friendship had officially ended. Anytime Anjelica caught Gerald staring at her she'd scoff and turn away. Gerald's heart sank a little more with every passing day and each icy glare.

Gerald kept trying to apologize. In every class, between classes, at lunch, at recess, before and after school. Every time he got close she left. He knew he screwed up. He was sincerely sorry. He would do anything to earn her forgiveness.

One day, during recess, Gerald approached Anjelica on the playground. Per usual, the moment she saw him approaching she headed the other direction. This time, instead of standing there dejected as he watched her leave, Gerald followed behind her, persistently trying to get her attention.

"I'm sorry. I didn't mean to."

"Well that makes it all better. You're completely forgiven."

"Anje."

She stopped in her tracks and turned to face him. The scowl on her face nearly brought Gerald to his knees.

"Do you know how much you hurt me? How embarrassed I was to see you staring at me like a piece of meat? I thought you respected me. I thought you actually gave a dam about my feelings. But you're no better than everyone else."

Anjelica turned around and stomped away. This time Gerald didn't give chase. Why would he? What could he say? She had every right to walk away. He didn't deserve forgiveness. Still, he couldn't stand there doing nothing while she walked away from years of friendship. Not if he had any chance of saving it.

"I wet the bed!"

The entire school fell silent. Not only did Anjelica stop in her tracks, every student and teacher on the playground stood still and silent.

"I wear pullups to bed every night because I keep peeig in my sleep."

Anjelica turned to Gerald in disbelief. Was he really telling the truth? Why would he lie? Even if it was a lie he told that lie in front of the entire school. Did he forget where they were? No. It wasn't an accident. He made that announcement in front of god and everyone knowing it would make him the butt of every joke till the end of the year.

The next day Gerald showed up to school and there was a diaper on his desk. The day after that someone left a puddle of warm water in his chair. No matter how many pranks he suffered through Gerald never said a word. They honestly didn't bother him. What hurt the most was the fact that his plan failed. He went another two weeks without hearing Anjelica's voice.

More than a month passed and, despite various phone calls home and multiple parent/teacher conferences, Gerald was still getting pranked. He showed up to school and there was a blanket soaked in lemonade resting on his desk. He tossed it aside and took his seat. He rested both arms on the desk and buried his face in them, desperately fighting to hold the tears in. He heard footsteps. A soft voice said, "Hi." Gerald raised his head and saw Anjelica standing beside him.

"Hi."

Gerald's heart beat faster. He hesitated. There was happiness welling up inside him but he didn't know for sure whether or not this interaction would be a positive one.

"Why don't you say anything?"

"About what?"

"You're being bullied Gerald. You should complain. Get them in trouble."

"I don't mind."

"You should. I know what you're going through. I know how much it hurts."

"I know you do. That's why I don't mind that they're doin' it to me. Cause now they're leavin' you alone."

Gerald looked up at Anjelica with sad eyes. Before she knew what had come over her she'd thrown her arms around him.

"You're a better friend than I deserve."

Gerald didn't feel that way. It wasn't an act of kindness. It was penance. He did something to upset her and this was how he evened things out. A better friend wouldn't have hurt her in the first place. If she hadn't forgiven him he never would've forgiven himself.

No matter the motivation, Gerald's actions brought Anjelica back into his life. She stayed by his side till the end of fourth grade, all through the summer, and all through the fifth grade. No matter what other friends entered their lives they always made sure to include each other. They celebrated every high and comforted each other during every low.

In January, a few days before winter break ended and everyone returned to school, Anjelica's family was in an accident. Her mother was five months pregnant. On the way back from the gynecologist someone ran a red light and smashed into their car.

Anjelica had a huge gash on the top of her head. She needed eight stitches. Her father had a broken leg and wore a cast for the next four months. Her mother had multiple internal injuries. Broken bones, ruptured spleen, punctured lungs. She died before the ambulance arrived.

A week after the crash Gerald was invited to her house. He knocked on the door and waited a few minutes before it opened. Anjelica's father was still learning how to move around with crutches.

"Hey Mr. Ramos. Is Anjelica here?"

"She hasn't left her room since we got back from the hospital."

"How is she?"

"Honestly…I don't know. She hasn't said a word to me. She's barely eating, barely sleeping. Barely crying."

Mr. Ramos stepped aside. Gerald eased past him and headed up the stairs. As he approached Anjelica's door he saw it was cracked open just a tiny bit. He pressed his head against the frame and peeked inside. Anjelica was sitting on the edge of the bed with her head drooping.

Gerald reached for the door, pausing with his fingertips nanometers away from the knob. What could he say at a time like this? No words would ever bring her mother back. Still, saying nothing at all would be even worse. He wanted to be there for her…even if being there is all he could do. Gerald lightly tapped on the door, then pushed it open without waiting for a response.

"Hey."

Anjelica was shocked to hear a voice other than her father's. When she lifted her head and saw Gerald she wiped her face on her sleeves and brushed the hair back from her face.

"Hey. What are you doing here?"

"Nothing. I just…can I come in?"

Anjelica nodded and slid over a bit. Gerald cautiously stepped forward and nervously dropped down in the empty space beside her. His gaze never moved from Anjelica. He was searching his mind for the right words to say. He never found them.

"My mom died."

Her words caught Gerald of guard. He wasn't sure what to expect, but, he certainly wouldn't have guessed that. The words weren't said with any hint of sorrow or anger. She was just stating a fact.

"I know. I'm sorry."

Gerald placed a hand on her back. She leaned down to rest her head on his shoulder. He slid his hand over to her opposite shoulder and squeezed her arm.

"She was pregnant. It was a boy. They were gonna name him Xavier."

Anjelica wrapped her arms around Gerald's stomach and buried her face in his chest. Gerald wrapped both arms around her, pulling her close and holding her tight while she cried.

"There's something wrong with me."

"Why?"

"Because I'm relieved."

Anjelica pulled back and Gerald saw her face covered in tears and boogers.

"My mom died. My little brother died. And all I can think about is how happy I am that I didn't die. How messed up is that?"

Gerald held her face in his hands.

"You're allowed to treasure your own life."

"No I'm not! My mom just died and my dad is miserable. I should be miserable too."

Gerald wiped some tears from her cheeks.

"You are miserable"

"No I'm not."

"Yes you are. I mean, look at you Anje. You're a total mess. You're sad that your mom is dead, happy to be angry, angry at yourself for being happy, confused because you're feeling all these different emotions at once.

Anjelica started crying again and buried her face in Gerald's chest. Gerald kissed the top of her head.

"You can feel more than one emotion at the same time. They're all valid. Feeling a sense of relief doesn't negate the sadness."

"How did you get so smart?"

"I don't know. I guess when you've been through some shit yourself it's easy to understand when someone else is going through something similar."

Anjelica pulled back to look up at Gerald.

"Did you lose someone you love?"

Gerald said nothing. Just smiled at her. He stuck his hand underneath his shirt then used it to wipe down Anjelica's face. He held it under her nose and told her to blow. To her own shock, she did blow. Then she looked down at the disgusting mess she left.

"I'm sorry. I ruined your shirt."

"It's ok. It's just a shirt. I've got plenty of others."

He was lying of course. He was wearing his favorite shirt and it was one of a kind.

"When the car hit us my life flashed before my eyes. But it wasn't the life I already lived, it was the life I wasn't gonna live. My first date. My first kiss. The school dance. Prom Queen. Learning to drive. I'm really looking forward to high school."

"Seems like you got your whole life planned out."

Anjelica stared at Gerald. He had no clue what was going on in her mind. She closed her eyes and leaned towards him with her lips puckered. He leaned back.

"What are you doing?"

"I don't wanna die before I have my first kiss."

"But you didn't die Anje. You're still here. You should make the most of every day."

"That's what I'm doing. Gerald…I don't know when I'm gonna die. Could be when I'm 100. Could be tomorrow. So I wanna go ahead and check one thing off my list."

"You're not dying anytime soon Anje."

"You can't make that promise"

Gerald stared in her eyes. He saw everything she was feeling. So much pain. So much anger. So much fear. He wanted to make it all stop. Maybe this was the way.

"Just shut up and kiss me already."

"Your first kiss isn't something you should do with just anybody. It should be someone special. Someone you love."

"I know Gerald. That's why I asked you."

Gerald's heart skipped a beat. He swallowed a lump in his throat and tried to catch his breath. Anjelica reached out and grabbed Gerald's hands. They both leaned forward until their lips were pressed against each other's.

For Anjelica, it was very anticlimactic. She was expecting magic; fireworks. All she felt was discomfort. For Gerald, well, they were the three most exciting seconds of his life. A memory to cherish forever.

Chapter 3

6th Grade

Towards the end of summer Gerald and Anjelica were busy preparing to enter the dangerous world of middle school. Gerald had been steadily growing taller every year and finally stood eye to eye with Anjelica. Speaking of eyes, he went to the optometrist who said he needed glasses…which Gerald lost after only a few days. His mom refused to buy a second pair, saying she wouldn't spend money on them if he wouldn't take care of them properly.

With the exception of history and gym Gerald and Anjelica had all the same classes together. That made their transition much easier. They didn't have to worry too much about making new friends or joining any clubs since they could lean on each other.

The workload increased but they were both intelligent kids who had no problem keeping up. The most stressful thing about the new school was the overbearing societal pressure. Gerald felt it weighing down on him much heavier than Anjelica did. To him it felt like everything he said, did or wore was always wrong. Anjelica had the exact opposite problem. Too many people liked her.

Teachers loved that she was smart, eager and attentive. Boys loved that she was cute and kind. Girls loved her fun and caring nature. Everyone in the school seemed drawn to her like a magnet. With each passing day Anjelica's sphere of friends continuously expanded. She was spending more time at the mall, the movies, at sleepovers…and less time with Gerald.

Before he realized it Gerald had become the weirdo loser freak picked on by students and ignored by teachers. To make matters worse, Anjelica would always defend him. That made people pick on him even more. When Anjelica was around they pretended to treat him nicely. When she wasn't watching they tortured him relentlessly.

Despite how horrible his life was at school, home was still a far scarier place for Gerald. The older he got the more violent his mother grew. Every time Gerald got in a fight at school, despite the fact that he was the one attacked and injured, his mother would punish him. All he could do was accept the beating. With both the bullies and his mother, fighting back only made them angry. They hit harder when they were angry.

The first time Gerald struck back against his mother she responded by grabbing a frying pan and smacking him across the face. He was knocked to the floor with tears in his eyes and blood in his mouth from biting his tongue.

When his mom saw the blood on the floor she smacked him again, told him to stop making a mess. He just laid there waiting, for her to stop yelling. Once she left he picked himself up, walked to his room, slamming the door shut behind him and locking it. Then he turned his radio on and laid face down on the bed crying is eyes out.

A few months into the year the school was holding a dance. Anjelica was super excited for her first ever school dance. She'd been looking forward to it all year. The morning tickets went on sale she ran up to Gerald who was standing at his locker.

"Are you as excited as I am?"

"About what?"

"Our first middle school dance. Have you asked anyone yet?"

"Nope."

"I get it. Fly solo and pick up someone there."

"I'm not goin'."

Anjelica was blown back by his statement.

"What? Why not?"

"It's not my thing."

"It's our first middle school dance. It's everyone's thing."

"Not mine."

Gerald closed his locker and flung his backpack over one shoulder.

"I know what it is. You're worried the girl you like won't say yes."

"I guarantee no one will say yes cause I'm not asking anyone cause I'm not goin'."

Gerald tried to walk away but Anjelica grabbed his arm and spun him around.

"Come on. You have to go."

"I don't have to do anything."

"But if you don't go who will be my date?"

What would be a better way to describe how Gerald felt? Perplexed or befuddled? Both fit but if I had to make the choice I'd say befuddled is a slightly more accurate description.

"You serious?"

"Of course I am."

"Why me?"

"Cause you're my best friend. I'd be too nervous to go with anyone else. Too much pressure. Plus, I really don't wanna sit around waiting for someone to ask me out."

Gerald turned his head to the side, trying his best to keep a stone face so Anjelica couldn't see how excited he was. He liked the idea of being her date. He also knew it was a slippery slope he was headed towards. What kind of life woud he live if Anjelica realized she could control every decision he made just by batting her eyelashes?

"I really, really, don't wanna go."

Anjelica sighed, feeling a bit defeated.

"Well, can you at least think about it a little more before you give a definite no?"

Gerald took in a deep breath and let it out slowly.

"I'll consider it."

Despite his outward demeanor, Gerald was leaping for joy. His heart frolicked like a deer through the field. He just got asked out on a date. The girl he liked wanted to take him to the dance. He was embarrassed by how happy he felt. Unfortunately, there's nothing in this world quite so fleeting as happiness.

The next morning Gerald was once again grabbing some books out of his locker when Anjelica approached him. He stayed up late last night planning how to break the news to her. He'd tilt his head to the side and say with a cocky smile that "If I got nothin' better to do that night then I guess I don't mind takin' you to the dance."

Before he said a single word he noticed something was off. Anjelica didn't have the usual bounce in her step. Her smile wasn't quite as bright. In fact, it seemed a little forced.

"Hey Gerald."

He wanted to ask her what was wrong. What could he do to fix it? If she told him to get water from the moon he would.

"Sup?"

"Um…listen…about the dance…"

"I'll go."

All the color left her face.

"What?"

"I've thought about it, and, you're right. I shouldn't miss out on important life milestones. I mean, you only get one chance to go to your first middle school dance. And there are worse ways to spend a night than with your best friend."

Anjelica's smile widened just a bit. You could tell there was some sincere joy behind it. There was also a hint of pain and guilt which could not be ignored.

"That's great Gerald."

She hung her head, her face drooping, and started walking away. Gerald was torn. He didn't know exactly what was going on, but he knew that letting her walk away was wrong.

He also knew that stopping her from leaving was bad news for him.

"What's wrong?"

Anjelica spun around.

"Wrong? Why would you think anything's wrong?"

Gerald closed his locker and walked up to her.

"Tell me."

"It's nothing, I swear. It's just that, well, Warren Griffin asked me to go to the dance with him…and I kinda said yes."

Gerald's shoulders slumped a little bit.

"Oh."

"I'm so sorry Gerald. I didn't mean to hurt you. Warren's just so cute and I never expected him to like me back so when he asked me out I kinda just forget that I already asked you but then I remembered and I made a mental note to talk to you about it."

As disappointed as Gerald was to hear all that he was equally impressed by the fact that she could say so many words in a single breath. That takes skill.

"But don't worry, I'll fix this. I'll go find him right now and tell him I already asked you first. I'm so, so, so, so, so so sorry Gerald."

Gerald turned around and covered his face. He seemed to be sobbing at first, then Anjelica took a closer look.

"Are you…are you laughing?"

Gerald turned around with a cocky half smile on his face. Anjelica wasn't sure how to feel.

"I already knew about Warren."

Anjelica's eyebrows lifted.
"What?"
"Come on Anje. This is middle school. Three seconds after you said yes the entire school knew."
"Then why'd you say you wanted to go?" "I'm sorry. I thought it'd be funny. And you know what, it kinda was."
"Gerald."
Anjelica playfully punches his arm.
"You scared me half to death."
"You take everything way too seriously."
Anjelica looked at Gerald stern but somewhat frightened.
"So you're really not upset?"
"Of course not. I already told you I wasn't gonna go."
"You should go. I think you'd regret missing it."
"Doubt it."
"Come on."
"Why is this so important to you?"
"Because you're my best friend. I want us to share this important experience together."
In his heart Gerald knew that nothing good could happen from agreeing to go to the dance. Still, after seeing the look of sincere pain in Anjelica's eyes when he said he wouldn't go…he couldn't stand the thought of disappointing her.
"Ok, fine. I'll go to the stupid dance."
"Really?"
"Yeah really."
Anjelica gave him a hug.

"I promise to save you a dance. Not a slow one though. That would be weird."

Gerald kept smiling as Anjelica walked away. The moment she was out of sight he slammed his forehead into a locker. He screwed up. He should've said yes the moment she asked. Why'd he try to play it cool? Playing it cool has never worked before. Not once in his life.

Over the weekend Anjelica's father took her to the mall to buy a new dress. She'd worn dresses before but this was the first time she'd ever picked one out for herself. As she kept getting older she would also have to learn to buy her own bras. Her father had no idea what he was doing…but he was there. He tried his best. Anjelica was always grateful for that.

Friday, the day of the dance, Anjelica was the happiest girl on the planet. Once again, nothing in this world is as fleeting as happiness. That afternoon, when she saw Warren in the hallway, she approached him hoping to confirm their plans for the night.

"Hey Warren."

"Oh. Hey Anje."

"So what time are you picking me up?"

"Ummmm…"

"You did buy the tickets right? You didn't forget?"

Warren started rubbing the back of his neck.

"Yeah, um, I bought the tickets. But…I'm not picking you up."

"Oh? Ok. Well, then what time are we meeting at the dance."

"Umm…I'm not meeting you…I'm meeting Stephanie…"

Anjelica's stomach was doing summersaults. She felt vomit creeping up her esophagus.

"I'm sorry…what?!?"

"Yeah, ya see…I only asked you out because I heard Stephanie was taking Arnold. But it turns out she only started that rumor cause someone told her that I asked Hilary."

Anjelica bit her lower lip and fought to keep the tears inside.

"But we talked and got that all cleared up so now we can go together."

Anjelica shook her head.

"And you weren't even gonna tell me?"

Warren shrugged.

"Sorry. Guess I just forgot."

She couldn't hold them back anymore. The tears were falling. She tried to hide them but they were as clear as the eyes they fell from.

"Oh shit. Look I'm sorry. Stephanie was always my first choice. I just figured you were hot so why not ask you?"

A chuckle escaped Anjelica's mouth as she shook her head and wiped her cheek.

"Are you ok?"

"Yeah. I'm fine."

Anjelica sniffled.

"You know what, I honestly don't even care. It's just some stupid dance and you're just some stupid boy."

Anjelica pushed past him and hurried down the hall. She burst into the restroom where she locked herself in a stall and cried through her next two classes. Then she went to the school nurse and said she wasn't feeling well. The school called her dad and he left his job early to pick her up.

When they got home Anjelica ran straight to her room and cried into her pillow until she passed out. When she woke up, despite being hungry, thirsty, and needing to pee, she just couldn't muster the strength to move. She had no idea how much time had passed while she lied there. Suddenly, there was a knock on her door.

"Go away."

Another knock.

"I said go away dad! I don't wanna talk about it!"

"It's Gerald."

Anjelica's head popped up. After how casually she tossed him aside his voice was the last one she expected to hear. Her eyes darted around and she was dismayed at how messy her room was.

"Can I come in?"

Anjelica jumped to her feet and started shoving as much as she could into her closet, under the bed and into any dresser drawer that had space. Then she jumped back on the bed, fixed her hair and wiped her face.

"Come in."

As Gerald opened the door, by some miracle in ultra-slow motion, Anjelica found herself feeling subconscious about her body posture. She didn't want to seem too inviting but also didn't want to give off the impression that she didn't want him there. Make it obvious that she's not in a great mood while not showing how bad she actually feels.

Side note: why are you women so complicated? I've honestly spent my entire life perplexed by the inner working of your minds. The previous paragraph was based off an actual conversation which left me vexed.

Anjelica settled on pulling her legs in while loosely hugging a pillow and slightly slouching. After somehow taking two minutes to push the door open Gerald popped his head in.

"Hey."

"Hey."

Gerald took a few gentle steps inside, almost as if he was wary of frightening a small animal.

"I heard about Warren."

Anjelica scoffed.

"Sure you did. I bet the whole school knows."

"Well, I am the least popular person in school. So if I know, yeah, the entire school definitely knew an hour before I found out."

Anjelica let out a heavy sigh and fell backwards onto her bed.

"Thanks for making me feel better."

Anje felt something touching her hands. It was light, barely noticeable, so she suspected it was a breeze from the AC. After a few seconds the sensation didn't leave so she turned her head and saw two thin blue rectangular slips of paper.

"What is that?"

"Two tickets to the dance."

She grabbed them, balled them up and tossed them aside.

"I don't need those."

Gerald walked across the room and picked them up. He unfolded them and pressed them against his leg to straighten them out.

"Yeah we do. They won't let us in without them."

She threw her pillow aside and pushed herself up.

"Us?"

Gerald sat on the bed and held the tickets out to Anjelica.

"You said you wanted us to go together."

"That was before the whole Warren thing."

"Yeah, well, Warren's going with someone else now. So there's no reason you and I can't go together."

"I thought you didn't wanna go."

"I don't."

"Then why?"

Gerald reached a hand over and placed it on top of hers.

"Because I know how much you wanna go."

Tears formed in her eyes as she pulled her hand away.

"Not anymore."

She pulled her knees up to her chest. Gerald rolled his eyes and chuckled.

"Yeah you do. It's all you've ever wanted."

She shook her head.

"I changed my mind."

Gerald stared at her in silence, unsure of how to break her mood. Then, he cracked a smile and tossed the tickets in the air. Anjelica watched them spin around as they floated to the ground.

"Fine. We'll stay right here then."

Anjelica stared at Gerald wide-eyed.

"We?"

"Yes. We. You. I. Together. We."

"There's no reason you shouldn't go to the dance."

"I only bought those tickets for you. I don't mind going to the dance. But I also don't mind just sittin' here. Either way, I'm spending the rest of the night with you. So if you're not goin' to the dance there's no way I am either."

Anjelica smiled and threw her arms around Gerald. She spent the next few seconds crying onto his shoulder.

"I was really looking forward to this dance. I bought a new dress and everything."

Gerald put his hand inside his shirt and tried his best to wipe all the tears and boogers from Anjelica's face.

"Then what are we waitin' for? Let's go."

Anjelica took a deep breath in.

"You mind waiting downstairs for an hour?"

Gerald patted the top of her head.

"I'd wait two."

He got up and walked out of the room.

"Take all the time you need."

Once Gerald was out of the room Anjelica ran to her closet to grab the dress. She also grabbed a bunch of makeup and ran to the bathroom. When she walked downstairs Gerald was wearing a dark blue polo shirt and black dress pants. Still had on the same sneakers.

When he saw Anjelica in that blue dress with matching flats, her hair up in a bun, he couldn't believe how amazing she looked. Was it even possible for any girl to look that good?

"Wow."

"Do I look alright?"

"You look…..wow."

Anjelica giggled. Her father walked over and pushed Gerald's mouth closed. He stepped over to his daughter with a small box in his hands and held it out to her.

"These belonged to your mother. They were her favorite. When I saw the dress you bought I knew they'd go perfect with it."

When she opened the box and saw the two sapphire drop earrings it nearly brought her to tears.

"Oh my god. They're so beautiful."

She jumped into her father's arms and squeezed him tight.

"Thank you daddy."

"I love you sweetie."

"I love you too daddy."

When the two of them walked into the school cafeteria Anjelica worried she might be overdressed. Half the students wore the same shirts and jeans they wore to class. Thankfully some of Anje's friends loved having an excuse to dress up. A few of them managed to convince their dates to wear button up shirts. No ties or jackets.

Gerald spent most of the night sitting at a table by the wall, watching Anjelica dance with her friends. Halfway through the night she took a break to sit with Gerald and just talk for a while.

"Thanks for making me come Gerald. I'm having such a great time."

"Looks like it. Where'd you learn to dance like that?"

"What I do can't be taught. It's all natural talent."

She reached over and grabbed his hand.

"Why aren't you dancing?"

"I don't dance."

"Why'd you come to a dance then?"

"I only came here to get you out of bed."

"So you're just gonna sit here all night?"

"That was the plan."

"Come on Gerald. I know you can dance. You danced with me before remember?"

Gerald flashed back to that birthday party when he and Anjelica slow danced. Hard as he tried he couldn't stop the smile from appearing on his face.

"Yeah. I remember."

He turned his hand over and grabbed Anjelica's. Her smile widened as she jumped to her feet.

"See. I knew it."

She tugged on his arm as she stepped towards the dance floor.

"So get out here and dance with me."

Gerald was torn between actively wanting to spend time with the Anjelica and not wanting to embarrass himself so bad that she never wanted to speak to him again. Yes, his dancing was that bad. At least that's what he thought.

"Come on Gerald. Just one dance."

"Ok. Ok. I'll dance with you."
"Really?"
"Not right now though."
"Gerald."
"I promise that before this dance ends I will get on the floor with you."
"Swear on your mom?"
"I swear."
"Ok."
Anjelica released her grip on Gerald's hand.
"Sit there like a lump. I'll be on the dance floor. Come find me when you're ready."
"I will."
As she walked away Anjelica shouted at Gerald over her shoulder, "You'd better. Or else." As she headed back to the dance floor she noticed her friends over at the snack table. A refreshing drink didn't seem like a bad idea so she happily walked over to them. She hadn't intended to eavesdrop, but she got close enough to hear their voices before they noticed her presence.
"I know if that happened to me I'd never show my face again."
"It's her own fault for saying yes. How is she the only person in the entire school who doesn't know how hard Warren gets over Stephanie?"
"Then she shows up with that cheap dress and tacky earrings."

"And that loser was the only date she could find. She'd be better off coming alone."

Suddenly Anjelica felt like she couldn't breathe. A wave of emotions was washing over her. There were so many conflicting feelings she just couldn't sort through. All she knew is that she needed to get far away. So she turned and ran for the door. In her blind dash across the dance floor she bumped into someone.

"I'm so sorry. I wasn't looking where I was…"

She lifted her head and her eyes widened when she saw Warren's face. Worse yet, the self-centered prick saw the tears welling up in her eyes and assumed it was all about him.

"Oh jeez, I uh….I didn't realize you were that into me. I mean, listen, you're nice and all, but uh, you're just not my type."

Anjelica scoffed, rolled her eyes, shoved him aside and stormed out the door. Gerald, like most people in the room, didn't see the entire sequence of events. He saw Anjelica standing in front of Warren, then running out the door with tears in her eyes. What he felt could only be described as righteous indignation.

Warren walked to the snack table and immediately began joking with his friends about what just happened. Gerald stood up and started walking in that direction. Every step he took was quicker than the last. Before he realized it he was in a dead sprint. Gerald hadn't planned anything. His body was moving on its own. His mind was only along for the ride.

Gerald leapt for Warren and tackled him into the table, knocking all the food and drinks to the floor. Warren fell into a puddle of punch, broken tortilla chips falling around him. Gerald sat on his chest repeatedly punching him in the face until two other students managed to pull him off.

As those two guys were dragging him away Gerald was struggling to free himself. His flailing limbs managed to do a little damage. His foot smacked one student's face, knocking him back into someone else. His elbow broke the nose of a different student, causing them to stumble into an unsuspecting crowd. Then Warren got to his feet and tackled Gerald to the ground along with the two that were holding him.

Long story short, Gerald started a brawl. Once the fists started flying Gerald no longer cared who he was hitting. As long as his punches landed on someone's face he felt satisfied. He kept punching every face that stood in front of him until a school security guard grabbed him and took him to the ground, keeping Gerald pinned down by kneeling on his spine.

Through all the ruckus Anjelica was locked in a bathroom stall trying to calm herself down. She wanted to call her dad and beg him to come pick her up. She also didn't want all those assholes out there to know they won. Most of all, she still owed Gerald a dance. She didn't want to let her friend down.

She went to the sink and splashed some water on her face. After grabbing a towel to dry herself she looked in the mirror and realized her makeup was a mess. So she used a wet paper towel to try scrubbing enough off that it was even. She wanted to at least look like she did it on purpose. As she headed back to the cafeteria she witnessed a huge mass of students being herded out the door. Anjelica ran up to the group and grabbed the arm of the first person she saw.

"What's going on?"

"There was a fight. Teachers are sendin' everyone home."

Anjelica went to the office to ask if she could use their phone. She saw something out of the corner of her eye. When she turned her head she saw Gerald and Warren sitting in two chairs just outside the principal's office. Their eyes were swollen, mouths bloodied and clothes covered in multiple different stains.

It took less than a second for Anjelica to go from confused to shocked to pissed the fuck off. She called her dad, let him know what was happening, then slammed the phone down loud enough that everyone in the office jumped. Gerald looked up and saw the rage in Anjelica's eyes. He hung his head in shame. She walked out without saying a word.

Saturday morning Anjelica and her father were sitting down to eat breakfast when someone knocked on their front door. Anjelica got up to check who it was. When she looked through the peephole and saw Gerald she wasn't sure if she should feel shocked, angry or relieved. She didn't want to open the door at first. Then she took a second look and noticed that Gerald had some extra cuts and bruises. One eye was swollen shut and his nose was pointing the wrong direction. She tentatively swung the door open.

"Hey."

"Hey."

"You didn't have that last night."

She reached a hand out and touched a cut on Gerald's cheek. He winced in pain.

"It happened after I left the dance."

"Did Warren and his friends jump you?" He lowered his head and dug at the ground with his toes.

"Uh…yeah, sure. That's what happened."

Anjelica sighed, crossed her arms and leaned against the door frame.

"I'm gonna kill him."

Gerald titled his head to the side.

"Don't. You'll only make it worse."

"How can helping my friend make it worse?"

Gerald shrugged.

"It's a guy thing. We fought, he won, now it's done."

"So it's over? Just like that?"

"Just like that."

"Well why'd it start in the first place?"

"He made you cry."

"No he didn't!"

Anjelica stepped forward, her gesticulations increasing to match the ever rising volume of her voice.

"I was already crying before I bumped into him."

Gerald started scratching the back of his neck.

"You were?"

"Yes! I was upset because those bitches I thought were my friends were talking shit about me behind my back.

It had nothing to do with Warren. But thanks to you now the entire school knows that he did."

"I'm sorry. I saw you talking to him and you walked away in tears. What else was I supposed to do?"

"Follow me! Comfort the girl that's crying! Why is throwing punches the first thing that pops into your head? What good does violence ever do?"

"The revolutionary war. The civil war. Violence has led to some positive outcomes."

"Why do you have to be such a smartass?!"

"Better than being a dumbass."

"Right now you're being both!"

Spit flew out of Anjelica's mouth with every word she said. Gerald took a couple steps back and lowered his head. Anjelica paused for a second when she noticed a couple of tears rolling down his cheeks. She hadn't noticed that for the latter half of this conversation she had a scowl tattooed on her face and a river of tears flowing down each cheek. She stopped to wipe her face while Gerald was kicking blades of grass.

"Why'd you do it anyways?"

Gerald shrugged.

"I don't know. I just…I saw you crying, and I…I just wanted to make him feel as much pain as he made you feel."

Anjelica chuckled and brushed the hair back from her face.

"That's so stupid."

Anjelica threw her arms around Gerald's neck, resting her head against his. He nervously raised his arms to embrace her.

"Next time, just come to me ok. Fuck Warren. He's not worth wasting your time on."

Gerald gently rubbed Anjelica's back.

"Ok."

Anjelica stepped back and smiled at Gerald. He smiled right back.

"Did you eat breakfast?"

Gerald shook his head.

"Not yet?"

"Are you hungry? You can come inside if you want."

Gerald shook his head.

"I'd love to. But I'm kinda grounded right now. I gotta get back before my mom realizes I'm gone or she will literally kill me."

Anjelica giggled.

"Well, I don't want you to die. You better leave."

Gerald started heading down the street. Anjelica shouted out to him.

"I'll see you Monday."

Gerald turned around.

"Actually, you won't. I've been suspended."

"Suspended and grounded? You're basically under house arrest aren't you?"

"As soon as I'm free, the first thing I'll do is come see you."

"You better."

Anjelica stood in the doorway staring at Gerald until he was out of sight.

Chapter 4
7th Grade

Gerald and Anjelica spent half their summer together. That may seem like a lot to some people but the number was actually down from the year before. Gerald was in the middle of puberty, which made it difficult for him to spend any excess time with Anjelica. He randomly got erections doing math homework, how could he expect to keep it down when the girl of his dreams hugged him?

While Gerald spent the majority of his time indoors, playing video games or watching TV, Anjelica spent most of her free time having fun with the new friends she made last year. She had a fun summer filled with adventure and made plenty of wonderful memories. Still, she was excited to return to school.

Gerald was never excited to go to school. That year was especially disappointing. He and Anjelica only had a few classes together. Anjelica was placed in some advanced classes. Gerald was as smart as Anjelica, if not smarter, but he never cared enough about school to make any real effort. School awards you based on what you have done, not what you're capable of.

In addition to their different schedules they also formed different cliques. Anjelica could be described as the typical all-American girl. Beautiful smart, sweet and funny with a spotless permanent record. She was never late, much less absent. Never got a grade under 90. She seemed to make friends with everyone she said hi to.

Gerald only had two friends outside of Anjelica, a couple of stoners named Juan and Charlie. They sat behind him in English class having a conversation about Dragon Ball Z when Gerald interjected with his opinions. That discussion continued into the hallway long after the bell rang. Suddenly Gerald was hanging out with them every day.

Most days they'd go to Juan's house to smoke weed and stuff their faces while watching anime. Charlie was a skater. Sometimes Juan and Gerald would follow him to the park. They'd sit off to the side laughing and joking while Charlie worked on different tricks. Now and then they'd get bored with their monotonous lives and head to the mall to see a movie or play at the arcade.

Gerald never took any initiative within the group. He always went where they wanted and did what they wanted. He'd never done a single drug in his life before meeting them. Never once asked them to pass the joint. He was just so afraid of his limited options for friendship that whenever the blunt was handed to him he inhaled without hesitation.

One day Charlie brought up the fact that they'd never been to Gerald's place. They spent the majority of their time at Juan's, with an occasional trip to Charlie's, but never once went to Gerald's. Gerald told them his mom was too strict. They'd never get away with half the shit that Juan's mom ignored. That's why they spent so much time over there. As long as the house didn't burn down and there were no dead bodies Juan's mom didn't ask questions.

"Hey Gerald."

Saying Gerald had a heart attack at the sound of Anjelica's voice is a mild exaggeration. Still, it definitely caught him off guard. It had been months since he heard her voice. He especially did not predict the conversation that followed.

"Hey Anje. What's up?"

"How ya been? Feels like we haven't talked in weeks."

"Months actually."

"Really? Has it been that long?"

"We haven't said a word to each other since the first week of school."

Gerald slammed his locker shut and turned to leave. Anjelica reached out and grabbed his arm.

"Hey, you know the dance is coming up right?"

"And?"

"Did you forget?"

Gerald didn't forget. They went to every dance together last year. Over the summer they promised to do the same thing again this year.

"I remember. I didn't think you did."

"Of course I do. It was my idea."

"And you're actually gonna hold me to it?"

"Why wouldn't I? What's going on?"

"What's going on? You don't talk to me all year and now you wanna hold me hostage to some stupid promise just cause you can't find a date."

"For your information I've had plenty of offers."

"Then why are you here?"

"Because a promise actually means something to me. What does it mean to you?"

"They're empty words coming from somebody who doesn't actually give a dam about you."

As Gerald walked away Anjelica was devastated. She did have other offers. She turned them all down because she couldn't fathom the possibility of betraying Gerald again. Turns out she already had. Sure, he bore some of the blame. The phone works both ways. Still, she couldn't ignore, nor undo, the fact that she went two entire months without making a single attempt to contact him.

She could see through the angry words and violent posturing. She hurt him in the worst way possible. She forgot about him. She got a new life and moved on without him. From that point on they didn't even say hi when they walked past each other in the halls.

The night of the dance Gerald somehow found himself in the scarcely decorated cafeteria. He didn't know how he got there. Someone mentioned it to Juan or Charlie and they thought it might be fun to steal some food and rip on the posers.

They showed up with plastic bags lining every pocket and spent most of the night hugging the walls, occasionally walking past the snack table to discreetly slide some food into their pockets. During one trip to the snack table Gerald bumped into Anjelica. He would've liked to pretend he didn't see her, she would've liked to do the same, but they were literally staring each other straight in the eyes.

"Hey."

"Hey."

They both turned their heads away. Each felt awkward and wanted to leave, neither could find the courage to move their legs.

"Is this how it's gonna be for the rest of our lives? Pretending we don't know each other?"

Gerald turned to look her in the eyes, then turned his head away again. He couldn't think of the right thing to say. He was scared that the wrong words could make the situation worse...if that was even possible.

"Fine! Be like that! I don't even care anymore!"

She spun around, ready to stomp away, when Gerald reached out and grabbed her arm.

"Would you mind...saving me a dance?"

Anjelica's entire body relaxed, with the exception of her head which whipped around so fast it actually made a whooshing noise.

"Really?"

Gerald released his grip.

"Really."

Anjelica smiled.

"Of course. I'd love to."

Gerald smiled back.

"Good."

As she made her way back to the dance floor Gerald's smile faded. He stuffed a couple sandwich squares into his pockets then headed out the door. A teacher asked where he was going. Gerald said he was going to the restroom. The second the teacher turned his head Gerald changed direction and walked outside.

Gerald headed to the back of the building were Juan and Charlie were sitting on the ground, their backs against the wall and their laps filled with food, taking turns sipping from a flask. When they saw Gerald headed their way Juan held the flask out. Gerald grabbed it and took a swig. He barely managed to swallow the caustic liquid without choking.

"God, what the hell is this?"

"You've never had vodka?"

Gerald attempted to take a step forward and stumbled.

"Whoa. This shit hits hard."

"It's cause you got nothin' in your stomach."

As Gerald sat down Juan slid a corn chip between Gerald's lips. While Juan took a sip from the flask Charlie lit up a blunt.

"Where were you hiding that?"

"Same place I had the flask. In my underwear."

"Next time just lie to me."

"Don't act like you've never wanted to taste my balls."

The three of them sat there for about twenty minutes passing the blunt and flask back and forth between them while chowing down on all the food in their pockets.

The door swung open and Charlie quickly dropped the blunt into his pants. Gerald hesitated so Juan grabbed the flask from him and slid it into his underwear.

They all rose to their feet as the teacher made his way over to them. He leaned in and took turns sniffing each of them
"Alright, empty your pockets."

They all turned their pockets out and crumbs fell to the ground. The teacher let out a heavy sigh.

"Do I have to frisk all of you?"

Juan burped.

"I believe there's some sort of law against illegal search and seizure."

"If there's nothing to seize you won't mind me searching."

"If that's your evidence you've got a pretty flimsy case your honor."

"I think he just wants to feel up some young boys."

The teacher grabbed Juan by the collar and shoved him against the wall.

"Listen here you little shit. I don't get paid enough to deal with this crap."

The teacher opened his hands and stepped back.

"Go home before I call the cops."

"No worries. We outie."

Juan and Charlie got a few feet away before realizing that Gerald hadn't taken a single step.

"You comin?"

Gerald shook his head.

"Thought I'd stick around a bit longer."

"You know she's outta your league right?"

"I'll catch you guys later."

Gerald waved them off then walked back inside. He knew how ridiculous it was but the simple fact is: Anjelica promised to dance with him. He didn't want to miss his chance. So there he sat, patiently waiting at the table as the night slowly dragged on. Song after song he watched Anjelica on the dance floor surrounded by friends, laughing the night away.

A slow song started playing. Over the opening instrumentals the DJ informed the crowd that this would be the last dance. Gerald's eyes lit up as he watched Anjelica scan the room. Then, to his dismay, she turned the other direction. She found her date and dragged him onto the dance floor.

As the two of them swayed back and forth Gerald lowered his head, squeezed his eyes shut, clenched his fists and gritted his teeth. He knew exactly what would happen. He'd hoped she would prove him wrong. She didn't. Gerald rose to his feet and began the long trudge home.

"Where the hell were you?"

The only words his mother ever said any time he arrived home after her. Do other moms get mad at their children for having a social life?

"I asked you a question."

"Out."

"Out where?"

"At the dance."

"What dance?"

"I go to school. Sometimes they have dances."

7th Grade

She grabbed the toaster and flung it across the room. Gerald ducked down and watched it bounce off the wall.

"Don't talk back to me."

"You asked a question. I answered."

She lunged across the room and smacked him across the face.

"Don't you dare raise your voice to me! I don't know how I raised such an insolent brat!"

If you asked Gerald what he was thinking in that moment he wouldn't have been able to answer you. Maybe he wasn't thinking at all. He was just angry. Anjelica got a new life and left him behind. Pretty soon she would forget he even existed. The only thing Gerald felt was pain. So much pain. He wanted to get rid of it. He wanted to pass it on to someone else.

His mother deserved to feel pain. How many times had she hit him for no reason? How much pain had she caused him? How much blood did she make him shed? If anyone deserved to feel miserable it was her. Gerald balled up his fist, cocked it back then swung it forward. When his fist connected with his mother's cheek she fell to the floor like and anvil.

Gerald looked down at his mother, staring up at him with eyes wide from fear, shock and anger. At that point in his life nothing had ever felt as satisfying as that moment. He felt so powerful. Then the night fell. While Gerald slept his mother crept into his room with a hammer in her hand. She didn't bother waking him. She just started hitting.

"Don't! You! Ever! Raise! A! Hand! To! Me! Again!"

The pain of bones cracking woke Gerald. His first instinct was to raise his hands in defense. Once he realized what was happening he reached out to grab the hammer. After a brief struggle he managed to yank it from her hands and tossed it into the hallway. She smacked his face.

"I will not tolerate you showing me any disrespect."

She walked into the hallway and picked the hammer off the ground. She stood there glaring at Gerald for a few seconds before walking away. Gerald reached a hand up to his face. When he pulled it back it was covered in blood. One of his fingers was pointing the wrong direction. He snapped it back in place.

"Gaaaaaah!"

He didn't expect it to hurt that much. It never looked painful in the movies. He fell back onto his bed and took a few seconds to catch his breath. He decided to walk to the bathroom and wash his face.

"Holy shit!"

He turned the lights on and barely recognized his own face. One eye was swollen shut, throbbing like a pulsating grape. His nose was out of place, there was a big cut on one cheek. He cleaned off the blood and went back to bed. He couldn't fall asleep. The next morning Gerald patiently waited while his mom got dressed, ate breakfast and headed out for work. The moment she was out the door he locked the deadbolt, crawled back into bed and finally closed his eyes.

He didn't go to school for a few days. When the school called to ask his mother about the absences Gerald erased the message from the machine. Late that afternoon, as the sun was getting low, there was a knock on the door. Gerald approached cautiously. He only had two friends and never gave either of them his address.

Gerald looked through the peephole and was stunned to see Anjelica standing there. He wondered what she was doing there. What could she possibly have to say? She knocked again, this time shouting his name. Gerald inhaled deeply, squeezing his eyes shut. He exhaled then swung the door open. Anjelica gasped when she saw the cuts and bruises.

"What happened?"

Gerald hesitated for a moment, his eyes searching the ground for the answer.

"Car crash."

Anjelica reach up and hugged him.

"Oh my god, I'm so sorry. Are you okay? Is your mom?"

"She's fine. Not a scratch on her."

Anjelica stepped back and started rubbing the cut on Gerald's cheek.

"Hope that doesn't leave a scar."

Gerald smacked her hand away.

"What're you doing here?"

"What do you mean? I haven't seen you around. I wanted to make sure you're okay."

Gerald clicked his tongue.

"Like you care."

"Of course I do. Don't most people worry about their friends?"

"We haven't been friends for a while."

Anjelica was genuinely hurt by those words.

"…Gerald…"

"You didn't even notice I left the dance did you? This is probably the first time I've crossed your mind since you walked away from the snack table."

Anjelica's eyes started to water. She turned away. She knew nothing she said would undo the pain. Gerald went from anger to fear when he saw his mom pull into the parking lot.

"Don't ever come back here again."

Gerald slammed the door so hard it made Anjelica jump. She wasn't sure what to do. Accept his hatred and walk away knowing she might never again reconnect with one of the most important people in her life? That can't be an option. Before she made up her mind a voice behind her nearly made Anjelica jump out of her skin.

"What do you want?"

Anjelica turned around and saw Gerald's mom glaring at her.

"Oh. Hey. Sorry, I was just, uh…"

"Do I know you?"

"Yes. You do. I'm Anjelica. A friend of Gerald's. You probably don't recognize me. I haven't been here in a few years."

"Why are you here?"

"I just came to check on Gerald. I was worried about him?"

"Why?"

"Why? He hasn't been to school all week."

"He hasn't been to school!?!"

Anjelica saw the shock on the woman's face and realized instantly that everything Gerald told her was a lie. There was no car accident. Why would he lie about something like that? Especially to her? If there was no accident, how did he get those injuries? Anjelica looked back at Gerald's mom and her shock had been completely replaced by anger.

"Thank you for telling me. I'll take care of it."

She shoved past Anjelica, stomping inside and slamming the door so hard that it shook the walls. From the other side of the door Anjelica heard Gerald's mom shouting, followed by a loud smack. Anjelica pressed her ear against the door. There was a lot of yelling, mostly from Gerald's mom, then Anjelica heard some glass breaking.

As she rode her bike away Anjelica thought about all the times Gerald came to school with mysterious injuries. Anjelica never asked for an explanation. She figured he was just a typical boy doing whatever daredevil stunts young boys do. When she got to her house Anjelica saw her father in the garage working under the hood of the car. She walked in, leaned her bike against the wall and approached him slowly.

"Dad…"

"Yeah sweetie?"

"I need your help with something."

He lifted his head and saw the sadness in her eyes. He dropped his tools and grabbed a rag to wipe the dirt and grease off his hands. Then he grabbed a stool and carried it over to Anjelica.

"Sit."

Anjelica sat on the stool and he knelt down in front of her.

"What's wrong?"

Anjelica shrugged.

"I don't know."

Her dad chuckled and shook his head.

"You obviously have something on your mind."

Anjelica turned her head away. She was so unsure. There's no proof that anything wrong was happening. It's just a bad feeling she got. What if that feeling was wrong?

"You know you can tell me anything Mija."

Anjelica looked in her father's eyes and felt safe.

"If I had…a friend, who knew that one of her friends was in trouble, what should she do about it?"

Mr. Ramos took a deep breath.

"I guess that depends on what kind of trouble you're talking about. I mean…is it illegal? Could someone get hurt?"

Anjelica paused.

"I don't know if it's illegal…but someone's definitely getting hurt."

"Well in that case, your friend should definitely tell somebody."

Anjelica slumped her shoulders and leaned back against the wall.

"Thing is…what if the friend doesn't realize he's in trouble?"

"Unfortunately, people don't always know what's best for them."

Anjelica closed her eyes and raised her head to the ceiling.
"You know you can tell me anything right?"

"I know, I just…I don't even know for sure that anything is wrong. It's just…something is definitely not right."

Mr. Ramos groaned as he pushed himself back to his feet. "You're gonna have to walk me through this one."

Anjelica stared her father in the eyes.

"I think Gerald's mom is hurting him."

Mr. Ramos stared back at his daughter. She seemed genuinely concerned.

"That's a very serious thing to say."

A tear rolled down Anjelica's cheek. Her father wiped it with his thumb.

"For years he's been randomly showing up with weird cuts and bruises in different places on his body. Today he said he was in a car cash but his mom knew nothing about it."

Mr. Ramos scratched the back of his neck.

"What should I do?"

Mr. Ramos dropped his arms by his side.

"Gerald's never said anything to you?"

Anjelica shook her head.

"Then I'm not sure you should do anything?"

"What?!"

Anjelica leapt to her feet.

"My friend might be in trouble and I'm just supposed to let it happen?"

"Baby…you should always try to help a friend in trouble. The problem is you have no proof. And if Gerald hasn't said anything so far there's a chance he'll defend her against your accusations."

"But if she is hurting him then why would he protect her?"

"She's his mother. You can't help but care about family."

"So what am I supposed to do then? Just go on pretending I don't know what's happening?"

Mr. Ramos reached out to grab his daughter's hands.

"If you want to report it to the authorities I will help you. It is the right thing to do. But from what I hear, there's a good chance the only thing'll change is…you lose your friend's trust."

Anjelica trusted her father's advice. He rarely ever said the wrong thing. This time there was one difference. It wasn't about her. Despite the risk she knew what the right choice was. She couldn't just sit on her hands while her friend suffered. She had to at least try to help…even if he wasn't willing to help himself. Together, Anjelica and her father contacted child protective services.

Nearly two weeks later Gerald finally returned to school. Both of his eyes were swollen and purple. He had a large band aid on his cheek that barely covered the huge gash. Anjelica stared as he walked past her without saying a word. Never even turned to look at her. When he stopped at his locker Anjelica approached slowly, careful not to spook him.

"Hey."

Gerald didn't respond. Didn't even turn to look at her. He refused to acknowledge her presence.

"Did she do this to you?"

Gerald slammed his locker so hard the echo reverberated through the hallway causing everyone to stop and stare. He glared daggers at Anjelica, as if he was imagining those blades going through her skull.

"Are you mad?"

"You sent cops to my place."

"I had to."

"Had to!?!"

As Gerald stepped towards her Anjelica's entire body quivered. Tears welled up in her eyes.

"Gerald...I know how she treats you. She shouldn't be doing those things to her own son."

"She definitely won't win mother of the year but she's the only family I got. How would you feel if I tried to get your dad thrown in jail?"

"My dad doesn't hit me!"

Gerald flicked his arm out to shove Anjelica aside so he could walk past. In his anger he shoved her hard enough that she lost her balance and fell into the lockers.

"Ow! Hey!"

Gerald angrily marched down the hall, refusing to heed Anjelica's call.

"I was just trying to help! That's what friends do!"

Gerald stopped and spun around.

"I am not your friend! Next time you wanna help, do me a favor, don't!"

"Fine! I won't!"

As Gerald disappeared into the crowd Anjelica leaned back against the lockers, covered her face with her hands and cried.

Chapter 5

9th Grade

High school. The worst four years of my life. Thankfully, this story isn't about me. It's about Gerald and Anjelica. Gerald kept growing, stopped just shy of six feet. He grew his hair out for over a year then went to a barbershop and got cornrows. Seven thick braids lined the top of his head. He also got a tattoo. A ring of barbed wire wrapped around his left bicep. They were designed to look like the barbs were digging into his skin, drawing blood.

While getting the tattoo Gerald was convinced to pierce his ears. A gold plated stud in each lobe. From the outside looking in Gerald could almost be mistaken for one of the cool kids. Nobody beat him up or teased him like they did in middle school. They did still spread rumors about him behind his back. It was high school after all.

Gerald was athletic enough that members of the school teams asked him to try out. He was smart enough to get straight A's if he bothered giving any effort at all. Basically, Gerald could have been the perfect American teen if he cared enough to try. Unfortunately he read Paradise Lost and decided he was happy to accept whatever place in society he naturally fell into.

The only thing Gerald enjoyed about school was spending time with his friends. He showed up just often enough to avoid trouble. Completed just enough assignments to get a passing grade. Made just enough friends that he always had someone to talk to when he didn't just sleep through half the day.

Speaking of friends, we've made it to the fourth paragraph of this chapter without mentioning Anjelica. There's a reason for that. Gerald hadn't said a word to Anjelica since their fight in seventh grade. Though their friendship appeared to be long over Anjelica had not completely given up on the possibility of reconciliation.

In eight grade they had three classes together: English, history and math. That math class was the main reason Anjelica didn't lose all hope of being friends with Gerald again. One day they had a pop quiz and Anjelica didn't understand half the materials. Gerald was seated right next to her and was easily breezing through it.

Anjelica leaned over to peak at some of his answers. Gerald noticed. Instead of telling the teacher, covering his paper or even just ignoring her...Gerald titled his paper to make it easier for her to read. That one simple gesture was enough to assure Anjelica that one some level, no matter how minor, Gerald still cared about her.

To test her theory Anjelica started asking Gerald for tiny favors. May I borrow a pencil? Could you spare a few sheets of blank paper? May I use your eraser? Gerald never said a word, never looked her in the eyes, but he always handed her whatever she asked for.

When high school first started she didn't even recognize the boy who walked past her in the halls. Once she realized who it was she was so shocked by his new look that she completely forgot they weren't talking anymore and gave him a compliment. He said thank you. Not wanting to lose the momentum she tried her best to keep the conversation going.
"So I guess you've stayed pretty busy this summer."
"Not really. Most of this happened on the same day."
"I get it. One thing leads to another and suddenly you've pierced our nose and dyed your hair purple with hot pink streaks."
Gerald scanned the top of Anjelica's head.
"It wasn't me. I was talking about my friend Melanie. She couldn't be stopped."
Though the conversation was brief it was a positive step forward. The draw bridge had lowered. Gerald's guard was down. If she was tactful about it she could easily sneak her way back into Gerald's life. How wrong she was. If Anjelica asked him to Gerald would gladly have dropped everything else in his life to spend every second of every day with her. He didn't feel that way after the conversation. He felt that way the day before. The week before. The month before. The year before. She never knew just how much he missed her.
Gerald was never mad at Anjelica. He was mad at the situation. Mad at his mom for hitting him. Mad that of all the women on earth this is the one who had to give birth to him. Mad because even though Anjelica did what she did for his sake she was also the reason he defended his mother. If he

went into the system who knows where he'd end up. The thought that he might never see Anjelica again was scarier than any beating his mom could give. Most of all, he was mad that she didn't realize how close they came to losing each other.

Anjelica never thought about the next step. All she knew was that Gerald needed help. So she tried to help. She was being a good friend. Gerald wanted to apologize but didn't know how. The longer it took the harder it got. Days turned into weeks and soon he was so embarrassed he couldn't even look her in the eyes. So that day in high school, when they had their first conversation in nearly twenty months, Gerald was ecstatic. It felt like things might finally be back to normal.

Unfortunately for Gerald, Anjelica's free time was already fully accounted for. Most of her mind was occupied by a boy named Adrian. Just over six feet tall with chestnut skin, a thin frame but very toned and a flat top haircut with the smoothest fade you've ever seen. He had a smile that could light up the night sky. So charismatic. Everyone was naturally drawn to him.

He and Anjelica sat next to each other in history class. There was an instant attraction. At the end of the second week of school he asked Anjelica on a date. She said yes with no hesitation. Nearly responded before he finished asking. They had their first date on Sunday. Their second date exactly one week after that. By the time that second date ended they agreed to be boyfriend and girlfriend.

If you know what it's like to be a teenager in your first real relationship you might be able to guess where this story is headed. Every decision Anjelica made revolved around Adrian. Her entire schedule was adjusted to suit his needs.

Gerald was the first casualty. His relationship with Anjelica was barely on the mend. Once Adrian became part of Anjelica's life she completely stopped putting any effort into mending fences with Gerald. They would small talk in class and nothing more.

Gerald would tell you it didn't bother him, an obvious lie. He kept living his life, spending time with his friends. He'd follow Juan home after school to play video games and watch anime. Occasionally stayed after school to play basketball or football, sometimes even with guys on the school team.

Gerald's life went on without skipping a beat. He never shed a tear. Still, every time he was in a room with Anjelica, every time she turned her head his way and their eyes locked, he felt a tinge of agony. Every time she smiled at him, waved her hand and gave a casual greeting, it always felt bittersweet.

Towards the end of September Juan started dating a girl named Jennifer. Despite being two years older than them she was in the same grade. She was held back twice due to disciplinary measures. One day Juan and Gerald were hanging out alone when Gerald jokingly said, "You know you're basically dating the girl version of me right?"

"If that's the case you need to get your shit together. That girl's a mess."

"If she's so bad why are you dating her?"

"I have low standards."

"You have standards?!?!?"

"Of course. She has boobs and she likes me."

"Your standards are higher than mine. I'm dating the first girl that shows interest."

"Even if she doesn't have boobs."

"Even if she's got a dick."

"If she's got a dick she's a he."

"Not if she's got a pussy."

"If you have a dick you can't have a pussy."

"You can have both."

"You're fucking with me right?"

"Fire up the computer. I'll show you."

If you've ever been a teenage boy you know what happened next. If you've never been a teenage boy, lucky you. Try not to think about it too much. Let's jump ahead to the middle of October. Gerald was in the cafeteria with Juan and Jennifer. They were talking about Halloween costumes when Juan asked Jennifer is she would do a couples costume.

"If you ever say anything that stupid again I will dump you."

A stranger approached the table. A five and a half foot girl with pale skin and long, curly black hair dropped her tray on the table and sat down next to Gerald. If you asked Gerald what his first impression of her was he'd tell you he was mystified by her smile. That's a lie. He definitely wasn't looking at her face.

"I've met that one. Haven't seen you before."

"That's the boyfriend's best friend."

"Some people call him Gerald."

There was no love at first sight. No sparks flying. Gerald and Melissa barely acknowledged each other. They only spent time together because they happened to know the same people. Little did they know how much effort their best friends were making to push them together.

Any time the four of them hung out Juan and Jennifer spent most of their time making out. They'd often sneak off, presumably to have sex, leaving Gerald and Melissa alone. The two of them gradually grew closer over time. They even started hanging out together without Juan and Jennifer.

Over the Thanksgiving break Gerald noticed something. Melissa was on his mind every day. The mere thought of her put a smile on his face. When he remembered the moments they spent together her scent filled his nose. The only other person who ever made his heart beat that way was Anjelica.

When school resumed Gerald went out of his way to spend as much time around Melissa as possible. His exuberance did not escape Melissa's notice. On the final day before winter break the group was eating lunch together as usual. The bell rang and Melissa asked Gerald to walk her to class. He happily obliged. As they trudged through the halls together she caught him off guard with a seemingly simple question.

"So when are you gonna ask me out?"

Gerald stopped in his tracks, as if frozen by magic.

"uh...I, uh....what?"

Melissa stepped in front of Gerald and looked him in the eyes.

"You like me don't you?"

Gerald rubbed the back of his neck. Melissa stood there silently, eagerly awaiting his response. He couldn't think of one. She pursed her lips.

"You know what, forget it."

She turned to leave but Gerald grabbed her hand.

"I'm sorry, I just…I've never asked a girl out before. I don't really know how to say it."

Melissa turned her head back with a cocky half smile on her face.

"Ask me if I wanna hang out this weekend."

Melissa turned back around. Gerald released his grip and cleared his throat.

"Melissa, would you, uh…you wanna do something this weekend?"

"Like a date?"

Gerald smiled sheepishly and nodded his head.

"Yeah. Like a date. Or something."

"Not something. It's a date or nothing."

"Ok. You wanna go on a date this Saturday?"

Melissa placed her hands on Gerald's shoulders and lifted herself up. She kissed him on the cheek then whispered in his ear, "I'd love to." She bit her lower lip as she walked away. Gerald stood there with his mouth open, a bit of drool hanging down. He couldn't move. If he took a single step his pants would shrink three sizes.

From that day on Gerald and Melissa spent as much time together as humanly possible. The days when they couldn't see each other they'd talk on the phone for hours. They wanted their first kiss to be romantic and memorable so they came up with a plan. New Year's Eve Melissa was in the living room with her family. A few minutes before midnight she said she was tired and went up to her room.

"Really? This close to midnight?"

"You've already made it so far baby."

Melissa stopped at the stairwell to turn back to them.

"There are so many words I can use to describe this ritual. Benign. Outdated. Arbitrary. Fruitless. Either way, I really don't care. I just liked having an excuse to stay up late."

She raced up to her bedroom, closed the door and propped a chair underneath the handle. Then she opened her window, reached her hands out and pulled Gerald inside. They sat nervously on her bed, failing to start a significant conversation.

Downstairs they heard Melissa's parents counting down from ten. They locked eyes. Gerald's heart felt like a jackhammer to the back of his sternum. They leaned over. Their lips touched. For two seconds Gerald's heart stopped. After they pulled away Melissa laid her head on Gerald's shoulder and held his hands.

By the time they returned to school Gerald and Melissa were the most disgustingly mushy couple ever. Always walked down the halls with their fingers interlocked. Never fought. On Valentine's Day Melissa told her parents that Gerald was taking her to dinner. She bought a new dress, earrings, even borrowed her mother's heels.

Jennifer picked Melissa up then drove around the corner and waited for Melissa's parents to leave for their date. Then Jennifer drove back to the house. Melissa hopped out of the car and ran to pop the trunk. Gerald crawled out and the two of them ran inside and bounded up the stairs heading straight for Melissa's bedroom.

They planned this for months. It was the first time for both of them. There was some awkward energy. As they undressed they argued about whether or not to play music. There was some nervous fumbling around. Halfway through the condom slipped off. As they put on a new one they had a conversation about whether or not it was ok to have a conversation during sex.

Despite all that went wrong they persevered. When it ended they lay there, sweaty and out of breath, uncomfortable but at ease. The silence was deafening. They both stared at the ceiling wondering what to say.

"Hey Lis."

"Yeah."

"I think I'm falling in love with you."

Melissa Chortled.

"Dam. Was I that good?"

"No. I mean, yeah, but that's not why."

Gerald rolled onto his side.

"I've been feeling this way for a while. I figured, now's as good a time as any."

Melissa turned to Gerald and scanned his face.

"You're serious?"

Gerald nodded. Melissa covered her face with her hands and let out a low rumbly groan.

"Gerald...no."

Gerald's mind raced while his heart slowed to a crawl. A pit grew in his stomach. Melissa held the covers against her chest as she lifted herself upright.

"Gerald...I thought you knew this wasn't real."

Gerald scanned her face hoping to see any signs of deception. He wouldn't put it past her to pull this kind of prank because she's too embarrassed to say how she really feels.

"I...I don't understand."

Melissa sighed and ran her fingers through her hair.

"This was just supposed to be practice."

Gerald pushed himself upright.

"Practice?"

"Yeah. You know, we go through the whole thing together so we have a chance to try it with no risk. That way when we get real boyfriends and girlfriends we know what to do.

It's hard to accurately describe the whirlwind of emotions that surged through Gerald. More than anything else he just didn't want to believe the words she was saying. Did she really not know how he felt about her? Did she really not feel anything? How can the last three months be a lie?

"I'm sorry Gerald. I think I have to break up with you now."

Gerald didn't shed a single tear. He was too stunned to react. He just threw his clothes on and rushed out the door. A few days later he was shooting zombies at the arcade when Juan walked up to him.

"Sup."

"Sup."

"Haven't seen you in a while."

"Not since VD, when Melissa dumped me. That's why you're here."

Juan leaned against the machine.

"Look man, Melissa's a bitch. She shouldn't of used you like that. You're my boy. I got your back."

"Buuuuuuuuuuuuut….."

"But, Melissa is my girlfriend's best friend. If I'm forced to choose, I'm choosing the one who gives me blowjobs."

"I respect that."

Turns out, the only one who felt the slightest bit of discomfort was Gerald. Melissa wasn't lying when she said it wasn't real. She kept talking to Gerald as if nothing happened. He felt like a piece of his soul was taken from him yet he had to smile and pretend his heart didn't feel like it was being used as a pin cushion.

He spent the rest of the month walking around with his head down. When he finally lifted it…he saw Anjelica. He was sitting in history class when he noticed her walk in. She was wearing her glasses, a rare sight for her, she had no makeup on and her hair looked like it hadn't been brushed in a while. If she'd only looked like that on the one specific day he could've easily dismissed it. Everyone oversleeps at least once in their life.

Over the next three days there was no change. It seemed to be Anjelica's new permanent look. Her attitude was different as well. She used to be so bubbly. Annoyingly happy at times. Gerald couldn't stand seeing her so miserable. So one day, when he saw her sitting alone at lunch, he decided to sit across from her. Outwardly, she barely acknowledged his presence. In her heart she was cautiously optimistic.

"Hey."

"Hey."

Anjelica sat there quietly, gingerly poking at her food while Gerald stuffed his face. He stared at her, knowing he needed to say something, wanting to drag it out of her, feeling like he didn't have the right. She sat there patiently, silently begging him to drag it out of her.

"So...what's wrong?"

Anjelica fought to restrain her smile. She didn't want to show the immense relief she felt.

"Nothing."

Gerald looked down at his half empty tray. The look on her face perfectly fit the feelings he had after Melissa dumped him. He thought about all the things he wished someone had said to him. He couldn't guarantee it would make Anjelica feel better. It might not be possible for words alone to fix her broken heart. Still, for her sake...he had to try.

"I know we haven't really talked much lately...but I still care about you. I care enough to notice that you're hurting. I care enough to want to do something about it. I don't know if I'll actually be able to help at all, but sometimes just saying it out loud makes it hurt a little less."

A small smile started creeping across Anjelica's face. As she looked up at Gerald her eyes began watering.

"He was so perfect. So smart. So handsome. Funny."

A tear rolled down her cheek.

"Things started off so well. Then he got really possessive. Chased away every one of my friends. Kept saying everyone was trying to break us up."

More tears fell. She raised her arms to wipe them away.

"Turns out, they were. Because my friends love me and want what's best for me. I couldn't see how much of a jerk he was. But I didn't listen. I pushed them away."

Anjelica couldn't hold them back anymore. The tears were flowing full force. She covered her face with her hands and bawled loudly for a few seconds. She could feel every eye in the room on her. She wasn't being paranoid either. Gerald looked around the room. They were all staring. They were all whispering. She calmed down enough to talk but never took her hands away from her face.

"He expected me to be there for all his things. Got mad at me for trying to have a life outside of him. But when I did follow him everywhere he acted like I was annoying him. Like he was doing me a favor by going out with me."

"He's wrong."

That caught Anjelica off guard. She hadn't thought about it before but Gerald's voice had gotten deeper. More forceful. When he spoke with conviction he almost sounded like her dad.

"You're amazing Anje. You can do so much better than that jerkoff. I don't know why you ever settled for him in the first place."

Anjelica lowered her hands and looked Gerald in the eyes. He had such a stern face. It made her want to laugh.

"One day you're gonna find someone who understands how amazing you are and shows you all the appreciation you deserve."

She sniffled and wiped her nose.

"You really believe that?"

Gerald nodded.

"But I do have one piece of advice."

"What?"

"You have horrible taste in guys."

Anjelica couldn't argue with that. All she could do was laugh.

"Well what am I supposed to do then? Never date a guy I'm attracted to?"

"Exactly. Any guy you think is worth dating is definitely not worth it."

"So I just stay single the rest of my life?"

Gerald wouldn't mind that. They could both stay single best friends forever. What he really wanted to tell her was, "if you can't date guys you think are worth dating, maybe you should date a guy you don't want to be with. A guy like me."

"I'm not saying you can never go on a date again. Just keep in mind that if they seem too good to be true then they probably are."

Anjelica brushed the hairs from her face. She stared at Gerald as he drank from his milk carton and wiped off the mustache.

"I've missed you."

Gerald flashed her a quick smile before returning to his meal.

"So…what's new in your life?"

Gerald shrugged.

"Not much."

"Really? We haven't talked in months. You telling me you haven't been on any dates? Gotten arrested? Nothing?"

Gerald shook his head.

"Sorry. My life's kinda boring."

Chapter 6
10th Grade

Once Gerald and Anjelica reconciled they basically spent every free second together. As Anjelica returned to normal she began rekindling most of her friendships. Once again, Gerald got the short end of the stick. Over time they naturally began drifting apart. Halfway through the summer they lost all contact.

One night, near the end of July, Gerald was playing an online game on the desktop computer in the living room when his mother burst through the front door.

"Get off the computer. I need to use it."

"K. Gimme a sec."

"I said now!"

"I'm just saving my progress. Then I'll log off."

She stomped over and punched Gerald in the face.

"When I say now I mean now!"

Gerald yanked the plug out of the wall and held it out to her with a smug look on his face. She ran to the kitchen and grabbed a frying pan. She ran at Gerald holding it high. When she swung it down Gerald caught it, yanked it out of her hands and flung it with all his might. It soared across the room, crashing through the window and landing in a patch of grass.

She turned to Gerald and tried to punch him. Gerald caught her fist with his hand and held it there. She tried to punch him with the other fist. He caught that one too. Caught in his grip she struggled to no avail. When she couldn't break free she got desperate. She stomped on his toes and bit his wrist.

Gerald kicked her knee. It bent backwards and she fell to the ground crying in pain. As she writhed on the floor in pain Gerald felt an odd satisfaction. Vengeance at last. He wanted to finish the job. Grab a hammer and bash her head in till her blood soaked the carpet. One thing stopped him. Anjelica.

Gerald didn't know why but in that moment her smiling face popped into his head. The only thing in life he wanted more than killing his mother was to see Anjelica's smile. To hear her laugh. If he spent the rest of his life in jail he'd lose the only reason he got out of bed every morning.

He looked down at his hands. His fist were clenched so tightly that he could he his veins popping out of his skin. He fought to spread his fingers. His hands were twitching.

"Get out!"

Gerald looked down and saw a look on his mother's face that could only describe as pure unadulterated hatred.

"I didn't raise a son who would attack his own mother."

"You didn't raise me at all."

Gerald went back to his room. As his mother shouted obscenities at him he opened his backpack and held it upside down. Once all the books and papers fell out he filled it halfway with socks, underwear, shirts and a couple pairs of pants.

He walked back to the living room as his mom was pulling herself onto her feet. With one hand Gerald shoved her back to the ground and continued into the kitchen where he filled the rest of his backpack with soup cans.

"Stop stealing my shit! I paid for every single one of those! You have no right to take any of it!"

Gerald zipped up the backpack and flung it over his shoulder. As Gerald passed his mom again she was nearly back on her feet. So he shoved her to the ground one last time. As he stepped out of the apartment he slammed the door so hard he nearly ripped the knob out.

A few weeks later the school year started. Anjelica didn't see Gerald once that day. He wasn't in any of her classes. They never bumped into each other in the halls. A few days passed and there was still no sign of him. She tried calling his apartment a few times but only got the answering machine.

The more time that passed the more Anjelica worried. One week with no word was enough cause for concern. After two weeks she was outright frightened. One afternoon school ended and she was about to head home as usual when she spotted Juan leaning against a wall and walked over to him.

"Have you seen Gerald?"

"Not today."

"When was the last time you saw him?"

Juan shrugged.

"Bout a month ago I guess."

"Aren't you guys best friends?"

Juan shrugged.

"You haven't seen your best friend in a month and you're not worried?"

"Guys don't have to see each other every day."

"But an entire month and you haven't seen or heard from him at all? That's not like Gerald. Something's wrong."

"You've known him twice as long as me. If anything was wrong you'd be the first to know."

Instead of easing her mind Juan made Anjelica worry even more. So rather than go straight home she rode her bike over to Gerald's apartment. When she knocked on the door Gerald's mom answered.

"What do you want?"

"Is Gerald home?"

"Who are you?"

"I'm Anjelica. Me and Gerald have been friends since kindergarten. How come you never remember me?"

"Can I help you with anything?"

"Gerald hasn't been to school once since the semester started."

"And?"

"And? What do you mean and? He's a teenager. He's supposed to be in school."

"Why do you care?"

"Because he's my friend. I'm worried about him. Did something happen? Is he sick? Was he in a crash?"

"He's fine."

"He's missed the first two weeks of school. Something's not right."

"Mind y'own business."

Gerald's mom slammed the door so hard Anjelica nearly jumped out of her skin. Now more than ever Anjelica was sure something was wrong. She knew she couldn't leave this place without seeing Gerald's face. She started banging on the door and shouting at the top of her lungs.

"Gerald! Gerald! Gerald can you hear me! Gerald!"

"Go away or I'm calling the police!"

"Call them! Maybe you can explain to them why your son hasn't been seen in a month!"

Anjelica kept banging on the door and shouting, drawing the attention of the neighbors. Some assumed it was just some lover's quarrel, a jealous ex that wouldn't take the hint. A few of them poked their heads out to yell at her. Anjelica ignored them all and kept banging on that door. She was planning to yell until her throat collapsed.

After a minute the door swung open and Gerald's mom stood there with wide eyes and a knife in her hands. Anjelica shrieked then ran away. Gerald's mom chased after her. Anjelica ran into the street, nearly getting hit by a car. Once on the other side of the road she looked back to see if Gerald's mom was still pursuing. The woman was heading back to her apartment.

"Where! Is! Gerald!"

Gerald's mother spun around.

"I don't know!"

"How can you not know!?!"

"Cause I don't care!"

"How can you not care where your son is!?!?"

"I have no son!!!"

Anjelica stood there, stunned, as she watched Gerald's mom walk back inside. A frightening thought crossed her mind. She pulled out her cell phone and called 9-1-1.

"9-1-1, what's your emergency?"

"I'd like to report a possible murder."

An hour and a half later Mr. Ramos ran into the front door of the police station and ran up to the first uniformed officer he saw.

"Where is my daughter?"

"Sir, are you here to report a missing person?"

"No! I got a call that my daughter was here at this station. Where is she?"

"Sir, I need you to calm down."

"I need to know what happened to my daughter."

"I understand. But I need you to remain calm. Close your eyes and take a couple of deep breaths."

Mr. Ramos closed his eyes and took a couple deep breaths.

"Can you tell me your daughter's name?"

"Anjelica Ramos."

"Ok. If you wait right here I'll go ask around and see if I can send someone to get you."

The cop walked away and Mr. Ramos leaned against the wall. He sullenly watched the seconds tick off the clock until a man in a brownish beige suit stepped through a door on the other side of the room and walked over to him.

"Humberto Ramos?"

"That's me."

The man held out his hand and Mr. Ramos shook it.

"I'm here to take you to your daughter. This way please."

The man walked away. Humberto followed him through the crowded station.

"Why was my daughter arrested?"

"She wasn't arrested and she has not yet been officially charged with any crimes. She came here voluntarily to answer some questions."

"What questions? And what do you mean by yet?"

"There are some potential charges she could face. Filing a false report. Reckless endangerment. Disturbing the peace."

"Disturbing the peace? What the hell is going on? What did my daughter do?"

"If you don't mind sir I'd like you to wait in here."

The man opened the door to an interrogation room. Anjelica was sitting in there alone. She'd obviously been crying.

"Dad!"

She jumped to her feet and ran into his arms. He greeted her with a tight embrace. Then he gently pushed her back and held her face in his hands.

"You're not hurt are you?"

"I'm fine dad."

The man in the suit gestured to the table.

"If you don't mind, could you please have a seat?"

Anjelica and her father sat down in two chairs next to each other. The man in the suit closed the door and sat on the opposite side of the table.

"Your daughter freely admits that she made a false or misleading claim when she called the police earlier today to report that her friend Gerald had been murdered by his mother."

"What?!?"

"I didn't know what else to do. I wanted to make sure they actually showed up. And I don't know for sure that she didn't kill him."

Humberto stared at his daughter with wide eyes. She was speaking with sincerity. There was fear in her eyes.

"We brought the mother in and questioned her. She admits that on the 29th of June she and Gerald had a fight. He filled his backpack with clothes and canned food and walked out the door. She hasn't seen or heard from him since."

Anjelica reached out and held her father's hand.

"So what happens now?"

"Well, we're gonna charge her with neglect. That's about all we can do. There's a case for child endangerment but it'll be harder to make it stick."

"What about Anjelica?"

"She's got a spotless record. And she only did what she did because she was genuinely worried about her friend. And her concerns turned out to be valid. I can probably get the charges dropped."

"Forget about me and forget about her. What about Gerald? What are you doing about him?"

The man let out a sigh and slumped back in his chair.

"I've gotta be honest, there's not much we can do. We enter his information into the missing person's database.

After that, we just keep an eye out and hope we get lucky and someone spots him."

Anjelica leapt to her feet.

"You're not even gonna try to look for him?!?!?!"

"He's been out there a month. Even walking that's enough time for him to leave the state. We can't look for him if we have no idea where to even start."

Anjelica's eyes started watering. Her father held her hand.

"Is there really nothing you can do?"

The cop rose to his feet.

"A month is a long time to be alone in this world. Any number of things could happen."

The cop walked to the door and opened it. Just before stepping out he turned back to them.

"You're gonna have to acknowledge the possibility that you might never see him again."

He stepped outside and closed the door behind him. Anjelica dropped to her knees, buried her face in her father's chest and wept.

Just Shy of Serenity

Chapter 7

December 14th

Two cops in a squad car were driving past an alley when one of them spotted something and told his partner to stop. They put the car in reverse and slowly rolled backwards to double check. There was a man standing in a dumpster. He was black, around six feet with a short, nappy fro. His face was covered in stubble, his clothes dirty and torn.

The cops parked the car and hopped out. The man didn't notice them approaching. He was too busy ripping a garbage bag open. He reached in, pulled out some uncooked burger patties and started shoving them in his mouth. The cops approached cautiously, taking slow, soft steps towards him.

"Sir, would you mid stepping out of the dumpster please?"

The man looked at them and froze like a deer in the headlights.

"We're not gonna hurt you sir. We just wanna talk."

He stayed frozen for another second. Then his eyes darted down. He noticed one of the officers putting a hand on his holster. The guy dropped the bag and put his hands on the side of the dumpster. He swung his legs over and sat on the edge of the container, taking the plastic bags off his shoes. Then he hopped to the ground and stood there with his hands high in the air. Once he saw the officers relaxed, moved their hands away from their holsters, he bolted down the alley as fast as his legs would take him.

"Stop! Freeze!"

The cops pulled out their guns and fired a few shots each. The guy managed to turn the corner just as they started firing. The cops ran after him. They turned the corner just in time to see him turning another corner.

The cops holstered their guns and made a mad dash. They rounded the corner and saw the guy halfway up a chain-link fence. One of the cops ran over and grabbed him. As the cop yanked the guy down his arms were raked on the top of the fence opening huge gashes on each arm. He screamed out in pain as he and the cop both fell onto their backs.

"Get up! Get the fuck up!"

The cop lifted the guy up and slammed his face into the fence. The guy swung his arm back elbowing the cop in the face. Then he turned around and hit the cop in the face with a left hook knocking the cop to the ground. The other cop pulled out his gun and fired five shots.

Two of the bullets went into the guy's stomach. One of them hit him in the arm. One of them grazed the top of his head. The final one harmlessly flew by above him as the man fell to the ground. The second cop holstered his gun then walked over to check on his partner.

"You a'ight?"

The first cop rubbed his cheek as he rose to his feet.

"Yeah, I'm fine."

The second cop grabbed his walkie.

"Dispatch we need an ambulance. Hold for address."

As the second cop walked to the end of the alley to check for street signs the first cop noticed something. He bent down and rolled up the guy's sleeve revealing a tattoo. It was barbed wire wrapped around his bicep. As the second cop walked back over the first cop said, "Aw shit."

"What happened?"

"Look at his face."

The second cop glanced up and down Gerald's face.

"What am I looking at?"

"How old would you say this guy looks?"

The second cop took another look.

"I don't know. I'd say, early twenties."

The first cop stood up straight.

"I'd say about 16. I think we just shot that runaway."

The second cop stood there staring at Gerald.

"Aw shit. I think you're right. Aw shit."

"Calm down."

"Calm down? We just shot a kid."

"We?"

That night Anjelica's father sat down to watch the evening news as usual. There was a story about cops opening fire on a homeless teen who tuned out to be a runaway reported missing at the end of summer. Then, to Humberto's surprise, Gerald's face popped up on the screen. Humberto knew that it would be best if Anjelica heard the news from him first. He walked up to her bedroom and knocked on her door.

"Anje? You in there?"

No response. He knocked again.

"Anje?"

Still no response. He turned the knob and slowly cracked the door open. Anjelica was lying face down on the bed, headphones covering her ears, with a book open in front of her. Humberto walked over to the bed and nudged her. She looked up at him and slid her headphones back.

"Hey dad. Wussup?"

He let out an old man grunt as he knelt down in front of her.

"They uh…they found Gerald."

Anjelica leapt out of the bed.

"What?! Really!? That's great news! Finally!!"

Humberto swallowed a lump in his throat. Anjelica noticed the sorrow in his eyes.

"It's good news…isn't it?"

Humberto turned his head away.

"Daddy."

Anjelica knelt down to her knees. She grabbed her father's face in her hands and turned his head till he looked her in the eyes.

"Tell me what happened."

He saw the tears forming in her eyes. He knew that the second he told her what happened those tears would fall.

"Honey…Gerald was shot."

Her jaw dropped. Her eyes grew so wide they expanded her skull. The tears fell.

"Shot?!? When?!? How?!? Why?!?"

Humberto took a deep breath.

"Two cops found him rooting around the trash. They tried to arrest him and he made a run for it. When they caught up to him he fought back. They shot him three times."

Anjelica covered her mouth with her hands.

"Oh my god. Is he…"

"He survived. He was badly injured, lost a lot of blood. He was taken to a hospital and had to have multiple surgeries. They say he's recovering."

"Who's they? Who said it?"

Anjelica leapt to her feet and flew down the stairs. She slid to a stop in front of the TV but the newscasters had already moved on to a different story. She spun around to find her father trudging down the stairs.

"How come no one called us?"

"Why would they?"

"I'm the one who reported him missing."

"Maybe so Mija, but we're not his family."

"His only living relative doesn't give a shit about him. I'm all the family he's got."

She ran to the front door and shoved her feet into some sneakers.

"What are you doing?"

"I'm gonna go check on him."

"Not tonight."

"I've gotta see him!"

Tears were streaming down her face. She stood up and reached for the door. Her father lunged down those final steps and wrapped his arms around her.

"Let me go! Let me go!"

Her father had a grip like python. The more she struggled the tighter he squeezed.

"Let me go! I have to see him! Let me go!"

Her feet flailed around as she struggled with every ounce of strength in her body. Her father never loosened his grip. Not until Anjelica fell to her knees and burst into tears. Humberto picked her up and turned her around. She wrapped her arms around him and buried her face in his chest.

"I should be there. He's all alone. He needs me."

Ten days later Gerald was still lying in a hospital bed with multiple tubes sticking out from various parts of his body. Physically, he was healing well. He added a few surgical scars to go along with the ones his mom gave him. Other than that he was perfectly fine.

He was healthy enough to leave the hospital. There were two major problems preventing it. Firstly, they weren't sure where to put him. His mom refused to take him back. She signed some paperwork waiving all parental rights. Gerald became a ward of the state. They were in the process of finding somewhere to place him.

The second reason they wouldn't let Gerald leave is because he wouldn't eat anything. He was definitely hungry. His body was trying to eat itself. He just refused to put any food in his mouth. They had to pump nutrients in his body through an IV. He refused to talk to anyone. Refused to say a word to the psychiatrist who came in to evaluate him. He spent all day doing one of two things: Staring at the wall or staring at the ceiling.

When Anjelica first started visiting the hospital she wasn't allowed to see Gerald. Only family was permitted beyond the waiting room. Since Gerald didn't have any family he never had any visitors. On Christmas Eve Anjelica was at the front desk once again, her father right behind her, both of them begging and pleading to be let in even for a second. The nurse kept saying no.

"I'm sorry. If it was possible I would. But it's hospital policy. There's nothing I can do."

Right that second the psychiatrist, who had just left Gerald's room, was walking past and happened to overhear the conversation. Anjelica was on the verge of tears. The nurse was on the verge of calling security.

"Excuse me ladies."

The psychiatrist stepped in, interrupting Anjelica to pull the nurse to the side.

"I think we should let her in."

"Hospital policy--"

"I know what hospital policy states. Look…that boy is depressed. Physically, we've done all we can for him. I think seeing her will be good for his mental health."

"Hospital polic--"

"What's the point of saving his life if we just let him kill himself as soon as he walks out the door? His only living relative is his mother and she signed away all legal rights. He needs to know that someone cares about him. I'm taking her back. Tell on me if you want to. Saving his life is worth getting fired."

The psychiatrist walked over to Anjelica.

"Where is Gerald? Are you his doctor? I need to see him?"

"My name is Dr. Henson. I am a psychiatrist who's been monitoring Gerald."

"Will you tell me how he is? No one's telling me anything?"

The tears were coming down full force. Anjelica was yanking hair out of her head.

"My hands are tied. I cannot legally give you any information regarding a patient's condition."

Anjelica looked like she was about to say something so Dr. Henson held a hand up in front of Anjelica's face.

"However, due to his specific circumstances, I believe it would be beneficial to his recovery to have a visit from a good friend."

Anjelica's eye lit up. A smile spread across her face.

"If you'll follow me."

She turned to Anjelica's father.

"Sorry dad. You'll have to wait here."

Humberto nodded. Dr. Henson turned and walked away. Anjelica followed very close behind her as they weaved through the winding corridor. They stopped in front of a door and Dr. Henson turned to Anjelica.

"Before you go in there close your eyes and take a deep breath. I know you're going through a lot of emotions right now. But he needs to see a friendly, smiling face. Remind him that the world is a good place."

Anjelica closed her eyes and took a long, deep breath in. As she exhaled she felt her heart slow. When the door first opened Gerald barely acknowledged it. Since the shrink just left he figured anyone else to come in would be a doctor or nurse. Then he felt a soft, warm hand rest on his shoulder. When he turned his head and saw Anjelica a jolt of energy surged through his body lifting him upright.

"Anje?"

"Hi."

"What are you doing here?"

"I got hired as a nurse. I'm here to fluff your pillows."

"Seriously?"

"No. I came to see you. Obviously."

"But…why?"

"Why? Because you been gone half a year and I missed you. Because you were shot and I've been so worried that I could barely sleep and I wanted to make sure you're ok."

Tears started rolling down Anjelica's cheeks.

"I can't believe you'd even ask."

Gerald turned his head.

"I'm shocked you even noticed I was gone."

Anjelica grabbed Gerald's head and angrily jerked it back towards her.

"Ow."

"Of course I noticed. I was the first one to notice. I'm the one who called the cops and reported you missing. I'm the one who's been crying myself to sleep for months cause I didn't know if you were alive or dead."

He turned his head back again.

"You don't even care."

Anjelica was shocked. She took a few steps back.

"I don't care? I've known you as long as I can remember. You're the only brother I've ever had. I love you so much."

"No you don't."

"What?"

"You don't love me. You never have."

"Yes I do. I always have."

Gerald jerked his head back to her and glared angrily.

"I know you don't love me because I love you. And it's obvious you don't feel the same way."

Anjelica was silent for a few seconds. Her eyes were darting frantically around the room while she worked through everything he just said. Stunned by the revelation, angered by the betrayal, saddened by the misunderstanding.

"I do love you Gerald. I don't want to fuck you but I can't imagine my life without you. I think you're one of the most amazing human beings I've ever met. You're always there for me when I need you. You're one of the kindest, caring, most understanding people that's ever existed in my life. The only human being I care about more than you is my father."

Gerald turned his head away hoping to hide his tears from her. It was too late. She already saw them. She was crying too. They were both tear-filled messes.

"I love you Gerald. Why is that so impossible for you to believe?"

They both stayed silent while the tears continued flowing.

"My mother used to tell me she loved me. Then she turned around and punched me in the face any time she had an excuse."

"I'm not her Gerald."

"You're worse."

"How can you say that?"

"I've never been a priority to you. Whenever you have a better option you always choose them. Or haven't you noticed that the happier your life is the less you and I talk."

His words struck her heart like a sharpened icicle. She clutched her chest in pain and gasped for air. He covered his face with a pillow. She heard his sobs and every other emotion she felt was wiped away, replaced with only sadness and concern. She stepped over and sat on the edge of the bed.

"You're right. I haven't always been the best friend to you. But just because I'm bad at showing it doesn't mean I don't care."

She leaned over, rested her head on his shoulder. He felt wet droplets falling on his skin. When he turned his head and saw the tears in her eyes all his anger melted away. All the resentment he felt for his mother, towards Melissa and everyone else that wronged him, none of that mattered anymore. In that moment, all he wanted was to make her feel better.

"I need you Gerald. Please stay in my life."

Gerald lifted a hand and gently stroked her hair. He sat there, silently watching over her while she drenched his hospital gown. Hours later, when the tears all dried and Anjelica was long gone, the door opened again. This time a despondent Juan entered the room.

"What happened to your studs?"

"Pawned 'em. Needed cash."

Juan leaned against the wall and stared at Gerald.

"Visiting hours are over."

"I know."

Gerald chuckled.

"Rules never did matter to you did they?"

"They matter. But if I don't like 'em I change 'em."

"How'd you manage to change the hospital rules?"

"I didn't. I changed mine."

Gerald stared at Juan with raised eyebrows.

"I found out about your mom. That you were gonna be put in the system. So I talked to my mom. She's trying to adopt you."

Gerald felt his eyes watering so he took a deep breath in to try and stop them from falling. To some degree he knew Juan wouldn't care but he was still a teenage boy in a room with another teenage boy. Big boys don't cry.

"Nothing's official yet, but they're telling us there's no reason it shouldn't go through. So all that, combined with the fact that it is Christmas, the nurses decided to be nice today and let me come see my brother."

Gerald was shocked, excited, relieved, and overjoyed. He couldn't stop the tears from falling so he turned his head and stared at the wall. Juan wasn't sure what to do. He didn't know how Gerald would react. He almost expected anger. Maybe even some confusion. Not this.

"Why?"

The question snapped Juan back to reality.

"What?"

Gerald turned to him, his face a mixture of anger and confusion, tears still streaming down his face.

"Why?"

Juan stared at him in disbelief. Then he chortled and walked into a corner. He stuck his nose into a crevice and muttered quietly to himself for a few seconds before spinning back around.

"Look...I know you and I have never had the kind of relationship where we, you know, talk about our feelings and shit...but maybe we should. I mean...you disappeared. You were gone for a long time...and I was worried as shit. For all I knew you were dead."

Juan's eyes were watering. His voice started to crack. He spun around and put his hands on the back of his head while catching his breath. Then he slowly turned back to Gerald.

"We're brothers now. You can come to me. When you're sad...when you're happy...when you're scared...just say something. Say something to me. Ok?"

Gerald couldn't stop himself from smiling. For the second time that day someone went out of their way to make sure he knew how much they cared about him. Juan walked over to Gerald's bed.

"Well…I guess I'll see you tomorrow then."

Juan lightly patted Gerald's arm then turned around and walked out the door. Gerald leaned back, allowing himself to sink deep into his pillow. For the first time in his life he wasn't afraid to acknowledge that there are people in the world who sincerely care for him. He fell asleep with a smile on his face.

Chapter 8
11th Grade

The first week of January Gerald was pushed to the waiting room in a wheelchair. Don't worry, with the exception of a few scars he looked good as new. This was standard hospital practice. Juan and his mom were waiting for Gerald at the front desk.

"You look like shit."

"I got shot. What's your excuse?"

The ride home was a silent one. Gerald had been to Juan's apartment plenty of times. This time was different. This time he wasn't visiting someone else's home. He wasn't showing up for a few hours before dragging himself back to his own apartment at sundown.

From now on this is where he'd sleep every night. This is where he'd wake up every morning. He walked in the door and took a long look around. Everything was exactly as he remembered. Same exact couch sitting in front of the same exact TV. Same dirt socks spread across the floor. Juan, seriously, clean up after yourself. Those things are gaining sentience.

"Y'all want anything special for dinner?"

"Pizza."

"Nachos."

"Bacon cheeseburger."

"Chili dogs."

"How 'bout something you don't eat every day."

"Filet Mignon."

"Lobster."

"Something I can actually make."

"Enchiladas."

"Tostadas."

"Traditional or Tex-Mex."

"Tex-Mex."

Juan walked to his bedroom. Gerald followed nervously behind. When Juan swung the door open Gerald was shocked to see bunk beds pressed against the far wall.

"Those weren't there last time."

"You weren't sleeping here last time."

As he walked across the room Juan explained, "This room isn't big enough for two beds. There'd barely be breathing room. Much less walking room." Then he plopped down on the bottom bunk.

"Why do you get first choice?"

"Cause I lived here first."

"But what if I wanted bottom?"

"I can't have top. I toss and turn."

"So do I."

"You got shot three times. Falling out of bed won't feel like nothin.'"

Gerald settled in fairly quickly. He didn't bring anything with him when he moved in so he and Juan shared everything. It was shocking how quickly they ran out of clean underwear. The longer Gerald stayed the more his side of the closet filled out.

In the first three years of their friendship Juan and Gerald never had a single disagreement. After living together less than a month they already had seven shouting matches, three of which escalated into fist fights. Don't worry, that constant fighting was actually good for them. They grew closer than ever. One night they were sitting in their respective beds, reading comic books with 3 Days Grace blasting on the radio, when Gerald decided to turn the volume down.

"Hey Juan."

"Sup?"

"Whatever happened to Jen?"

"Whadda ya mean?"

"I haven't seen her, or even heard her name once since I got back."

"You were gone half a year. Things change."

"Well what things specifically? I mean...did you guys break up or something?"

"Yeah....something like that."

Gerald paused for a second.

"Sorry."

"Don't act like you aren't happy to hear it. You never liked her."

"No...but you did. So I am sorry that you're not doin' alright."

"I am doin' alright. It's been months. I'm over it. Even when it first happened I didn't really cry or anything. The two of us really didn't fit."

"Well I always knew that, but, what made you realize it?"

"Honestly…you were a big part of it."

"Me?" Gerald chuckled, "I wasn't even here."

"Exactly. You were gone. Possibly dead. Lot of conversations were had. Lots of thoughts went through my head. Part of me knew I didn't love her. But I kept trying hoping it might happen somewhere down the road."

"Yeah. It would be nice if it worked that way. Unfortunately, life is rarely that easy. You either love her or you don't. If you don't love her by now you probably never will."

Those words caused Gerald physical pain. The moment they left his mouth Anjelica's face was all he could see. A small piece of his heart died.

"You're right. If you're not into girls you can't force yourself to like them."

Silence. Gerald was scanning the ceiling, searching for the right words to say. He could feel Juan's nervous heart beating beneath him, pounding so loudly that it shook the frame. A small part of Gerald wanted to just turn the music back up and pretend he didn't notice what Juan just said. He was worried that would send the wrong message. Gerald didn't have anything bad to say. He genuinely didn't care. He was scared that if he didn't say something good it would hurt Juan. That's the last thing he wanted to do.

"Hey Juan."

"Yeah?"

"You never told me why you and Charlie stopped talking."

Juan chuckled.

"That was two years ago. Why bring it up now?"

"I don't know. It's just...you guys were so close. Then one day he was just gone. Never saw him or heard his name again. What's up with that?"

"I don't know. Honestly, things weren't that great between us when we met you. In fact, you basically saved our relationship. The only time we weren't fighting was when you were around. And when you weren't around, half the time we fought about you."

"Me?"

"Charlie didn't like that I always went out of my way to invite you. He thought I might have feelings for you."

"Did you?"

Juan chortled: "Of course not. You were just a great beard."

"You know, it's ok of you did. I mean, I never thought of you that way or anything, but I don't care if you thought that way about me."

"I know. I see the way you look at Anje. You dated Melissa for months and never once looked at her that way."

Gerald though about Anjelica. When he pictured her smiling face he couldn't help but smile himself.

"Hey Juan."

"Yeah?"

"Even before your mom adopted me I still thought of you like a brother."

"I know."

"If you ever need anything, I got you."

Gerald turned the volume back up on the radio and returned to reading his comic. A smile spread across Juan's face as tears rolled down his cheeks. He wiped them on his sleeves then picked up his comic book.

Since Gerald missed the entire first half of his sophomore year there were discussions about holding him out for the second half as well. Let him start his sophomore year next fall. Gerald fought tooth and nail against that idea. He wanted to graduate with his friends. After weeks of arguing an agreement was reached.

Gerald could return for the second semester, but was solely responsible for making up all the work he'd missed from the first semester. He had to do ten months of work in five months. Juan's mom thought it was ludicrous. How can they expect anyone to handle that kind of workload? Gerald only had one question.

"Do I have to ace the subject or is a 70 good enough?"

"You just have to pass."

Every morning Gerald arrived at the school library before they unlocked the doors. After school he stayed in the library till they kicked him out. He'd go home and study till sundown, then spend the entire weekend finishing homework and projects. It was a tiring but overall fulfilling endeavor. At the end of the semester his lowest class grade was an 88.

The rare occasions that Gerald would actually take a break to enjoy his life were entirely forced upon him. Every few weeks Anjelica would miss Gerald too much and drag him out of the apartment. They'd spend the weekend going to malls, seeing movies, or just chilling at the park to get some fresh air into their lungs.

Once school let out for summer Anjelica refused to go more than two days in a row without spending time with Gerald. Gerald was glad to have his friend back but there were times when it was a bit overbearing. Anjelica was acting like a mother who lost her kid at the mall and was scared to ever let him out of her sight again.

Occasionally Gerald, exhausted form over-socializing, would decide he wanted a break and simply not show up. That didn't work. Anjelica would show up and break down his door to drag him out of bed. Did I mention she got her driver's license? Made it much harder for Gerald to avoid her.

One weekend, about two weeks before the school year started, Anjelica drove Gerald to the mall where she spent nearly two hours dragging him around, making their way through every single store without buying a single thing. Their excursion ended at the food court with Gerald devouring a cheeseburger while Anjelica nibbled on a slice of pepperoni pizza.

"Did I tell you I'm going on a blind date?"

Sometimes having a face full of meat can be a blessing in disguise. Anjelica was so distracted by the ketchup drops on his chin that she didn't see the pain in his eyes.

"Oscar set me up with a friend of his."

Fuck you Oscar.

"It's weird going out on a date with a total stranger. But Oscar says he's a nice guy so I figured why not give it a shot."

Gerald hoped it would just be a shot and nothing more. How useless a thing hope is. Anjelica said it was the best date she'd ever been on. His name was Craig. Anjelica described him as the cutest, coolest, funniest guy she'd ever met. It didn't take two months, or even two weeks. Craig and Anjelica were boyfriend and girlfriend by the end of the second date.

The more time Anjelica spent with Craig the less time Gerald spent with Anjelica. It wasn't difficult. In fact, it took less effort than usual. She didn't ask him to hang out as much. He said yes very few times. Since he was never called out for making himself scarce Gerald assumed Anjelica didn't notice his absence. Then, one random afternoon she came bursting into his apartment demanding he spend the day with her.

"We haven't spent a weekend together since school started."

"And you actually missed me?"

"Of course. I figured it must be hard for you to be around me when Craig and I are acting all lovey dovey so I didn't push you. But I do miss you. So I've decided to take a day away from Craig to spend time with my oldest friend."

Anjelica grabbed Gerald's hand. The smile on her face made him want to cry. His life would be so much easier if she hated him. If only she found him completely repulsive. It would be so much easier to get over her if she was miles away rather than just out of reach.

"Ya know, if I set you up with one of my friends you and I could double date."

"No thanks."

"Why not?"

"I'm not in the mood for dating right now. I'm focused on school."

Gerald was no longer capable of making it through a conversation without lying to Anjelica. Mostly it was the same lie over and over again. He did want a girlfriend. One girl specifically. The girl right in front of him. It didn't seem right to date anyone else while he still had feelings for Anjelica. Wouldn't you be upset if you found out your boyfriend only dated you because he couldn't get your best friend?

For most of the year Gerald and Anjelica kept their distance. He focused on grades, she focused on Craig. They would hang out from time to time with weeks, sometimes even months, between each visit. He pretended he wasn't still in love with her. She pretended she didn't know he was lying.

Then it happened. The magical time that every teenager spends a decade of their life either dreaming of or dreading. Alright, I'm being a bit too overdramatic. Some people legitimately don't care. I never gave a dam one way or the other. Sorry, I got sidetracked. This story isn't about me. This story is about Gerald and Anjelica…and the prom.

Prom. You either love it, hate it, or don't give a fuck. Those are your only options. Nobody thinks about prom and says, "I like it, but I can live without it." If you care at all you probably care way more than you should.

For Anjelica, prom represented another rung on the ladder to adulthood. A milestone every person experiences only once in their life. Gerald saw it for what it was…a total fucking sham. First of all, how can you call it a once in a lifetime experience when you have two opportunities to experience it? Hell, if you're a hot girl you can go to four proms. More in you wanted.

The event is entirely overrated, overhyped and overvalued. Also, overpriced. Why are so many people that eager to waste hundreds of dollars, some even thousands, on outfits they'll only wear once to sit in an unnecessarily long car and go to a high school dance?

"Because it's prom."

"That attitude right there is everything wrong with America. If 'that's just the way it is' was an acceptable answer I'd be picking cotton on Craig's farm. No one should live their lives blindly following tradition."

"Gerald."

"What?"

"You don't have a date do you?"

"Never tried to find one."

"You can't be so scared of rejection that you never ask anyone out."

"I'm not scared. I Just don't see the point."

"The point is to make memories you can hold onto for the rest of your life."

"You can make memories anytime, anywhere. The brain is like a camera that's always filming."

"So why not make memories at prom?"

"Because it's a waste of time and money."

"Since when was spending time with your best friend a waste a time?"

"Since you're going with Craig."

"And Jenny. And Stacy. Gina's going stag. Bella too. You'll have a whole group of people to hang out with. And if you're that worried about being alone you can always bring Juan.

"First of all, I'm not worried. Secondly, Juan already has a date."

Anjelica used both hands to clasp one of Gerald's.

"Please? I really want you there."

Gerald looked down. The warmth of her supple hands was slightly loosening his hostilities.

"Why?"

"Why? Because you're my best friend. I want you to be there for every important moment in my life."

Dam you Anjelica. She knew exactly how much power she had over Gerald. She knew exactly how and when to use it. She knew nothing in this world could cause Gerald more pain than saying no to those puppy dog eyes.

"I'm sorry. I just don't want to."

Anjelica never said another word after that. Gerald assumed she understood how he felt and had permanently dropped the subject. He underestimated her stubbornness. At first, she said nothing. Life went on as normal. Then, the week leading up to prom, Gerald was at his locker when Anjelica walked up to him with one of her friends.

"Hey Gerald. You've met my fried Janice before right?"

When the girl next to Anjelica smiled and waved it triggered Gerald's spider sense.

"Sup?"

"Well, Janice was just telling me that she doesn't have a date for prom. I figured that since you don't have a date either maybe the two of you cou--"

Gerald slammed the locker shut, making Janice and Anjelica jump. He turned around to show the piercing glare on his face. A puzzled Janice turned to Anjelica as if begging for mercy. Anjelica's response was a nonchalant shrug.

"As I was saying, since--"

"No."

"What?"

"No."

"But"

"No."

"Gerald"

"No!"

"What the hell is wrong with you?"

"What the hell is wrong with you?!?"

"I'm TRYING to get *YOU* a date for **PROM**!"

"I told you I'm not going!"

"Why the fuck not?!"

"I! Don't! Want! To!"
"That's not an explanation!"
"What do you want from me?!?"
"I wanna know what's going on in that thick head of yours! You owe me at least that much!"
"I owe you nothing! I told you how I feel! You can't accept it because it's not what you wanna hear! It's not my fault that you choose not to believe the truth!"
"I can tell when you're lying Gerald! There's something you're not saying!"
Gerald turned around and walked away.
"You suck Gerald!"
"Not as much as you!"
"Go to hell!"
"You first!"
Anjelica smacked the locker then stomped off in the other direction. A dumbfounded Janice stood there, unsettled by the ordeal, unsure of what to do with herself. Anjelica and Gerald didn't say a word to each other after that.

When prom night arrived Anjelica and her four closest friends spent the entire afternoon together helping each other with their hair and makeup. Once they finished putting on their dresses and jewelry they went downstairs to endure a grueling three hour photoshoot from their parents. At least that's what it felt like to the kids.

Their dates arrived in a white stretch limo and were invited inside to continue the photoshoot. The girls rushed their dates out the door and they all piled into the limo. Everyone was smiling and laughing as they were chauffeured through the city. They arrived at the dance and everyone climbed out. Everyone except Anjelica, who spent half the ride staring out the window.

"Hey."

Anjelica turned her head to see Craig standing just outside the limo. He extended his hand out to her.

"You comin'?"

Anjelica nodded.

"Yeah. Yeah, I'm comin'."

She grabbed Craig's hand and he pulled her out of the limo. She took a deep breath as she looked towards the dance hall. Colorful lights, music blaring, plenty of teens in beautiful dresses and tuxedos. Her eyes started watering.

Gerald was in his room, laying in the top bunk with headphones on, listening to Natalie while reading Anne of Avonlea. He was so absorbed in it that he didn't notice the bedroom door swing open. He felt a tap on his shoulder. When he lowered his book and turned his head he saw Anjelica's face. The shock jolted him up onto his knees.

"What are you doing here?"

Her mouth moved but no words came out. Gerald realized his headphones were still blasting music in his ears. He took them off and stared at her. Her lips were glistening. Her face was a rainbow. She never looked more beautiful.

"Why aren't you at the dance?"

"Why aren't you?"

"I told you I didn't wanna go."

"Then I don't wanna go either."
"Bullshit."
"You callin' me a liar?"
"You didn't get that fancy just to come see me."
"Fine. I did wanna go to the dance. But I realized I don't wanna be there without you."

Gerald paused to scan her face, looking for any clues to her motives. He saw nothing but sincerity on her face.

"Why?"

"Why? Why do you keep asking that question? I told you already. You're my best friend. I wanna share all life's biggest moments with you. I can't be happy knowing you're here alone missing out on everything."

She stepped forward and climbed the rungs up to Gerald's bunk. Once her head was poking above the bed she rested her arms on the edge of the mattress.

"You only get one chance to make memories. I don't want you to spend the rest of your life looking back on high school and regretting all the things you didn't do."

She pressed her hands on the mattress and pushed herself up, then slid her butt over so she was sitting on the bed.

"Why are you doing this?"
"Because you would do the same for me."

Gerald turned away from her.

"What makes you so sure of that?"

"Duh, idiot. Because you already did. Don't you remember sixth grade? I got my heartbroken and decided not to go to the dance. You showed up at my house with tickets offering to be my date. I insisted that I wouldn't go and you looked me in the eyes and said 'I don't mind going to the dance. I don't mind just sitting here. Either way, I'm spending the rest of my night with you.' Well Gerald, I came here to tell you that...I don't mind going to the prom. I don't mind just sitting here. Either way, I'm spending the rest of my night with you."

She reached out and grabbed Gerald's hand. He held hers, rubbing her fingers. Gerald legitimately did not want to go to the prom. He didn't feel like socializing. He's never liked dancing. He had no interest in those memories Anjelica was promising.

He stared at her. She didn't put on makeup, jewelry and glitter just to sit in his room all night. Still, Anjelica was always very stubborn. Gerald didn't doubt that if he said no Anjelica really would stay there with him all night, listening to pop punk while reading his comics. That's why he absolutely could not say no. He knew how much she'd been looking forward to prom. He couldn't be the reason she didn't get to go. He took in a deep breath then let out a heavy sigh.

"I don't have a suit."

Anjelica giggled as she descended the ladder and ran out of the room. When she came back in she was holding a garment bag. She unzipped it revealing a light blue button up shirt and a navy blazer with matching pants.

"When did you get that?"

"Three months ago."

Gerald cocked his head.

"Are you serious?"

"Juan said you two share clothes sometimes. I had him try on everything till we found something we thought might look good on you. And that you would actually wear. Notice how there's no tie. I knew I'd never win that argument."
Gerald rubbed his tongue over his teeth.
"What made you so sure I'd change my mind?"
"I wasn't sure. I just knew."
"But what if you were wrong?"
"Then you and I would've spent the night playing the most expensive game of dress up ever."
Gerald chortled. Anjelica tossed the bag onto Gerald's bunk.
"Besides, how many times have you actually said no to me?"
"Plenty."
"And how many times have you refused to change your mind no matter how much I nagged you?"
"Twice."
"See. The odds were in my favor."

She turned and walked out of the room. She shouted, "Don't take too long. I'll be waiting in the limo." as she closed the door behind her. Gerald stared at the suit. He was starting to hate that part of himself. He knew it was wrong to live his entire life based on someone else's whims. Still, there was nothing he loved more than seeing Anjelica smile. That's why, despite his better judgement, Gerald begrudgingly put the suit on. When Gerald got to the front door Anjelica was standing next to Juan's mom who held a camera in her hand.

"I couldn't let y'all leave without getting a few pictures."

Juan's mom took a handful of pictures then Anjelica and Gerald went outside where the limo was waiting. Gerald enjoyed the ride, even poked his head through the moon roof. When they arrived at the prom they walked in the door arm in arm. Craig never said anything about it but anyone who saw him could tell he was upset to see his girlfriend with another guy.

Craig had no reason to be upset. It didn't matter who she walked in the door with. Anjelica showed up fully planning to spend the majority of her night with Craig. That's exactly what she did. For most of the night she was on the dance floor with Craig and her friends. Gerald spent the majority of his night sitting alone at a table, occasionally rising to his feet to walk across the room and grab some snacks or a drink.

Most people might assume Gerald's night was sad and lonely. Most people would be wrong. He enjoyed watching Anjelica spin around in her dress, wildly flailing her arms about. He enjoyed seeing Juan dance with his boyfriend. Relaxing in a comfortable chair, witnessing his closest friends living their lives with smiles on their faces...nothing could be more rewarding. Halfway through the night Craig meandered over to the table and plopped down in a chair directly across from Gerald.

"Having fun yet?"

"Obviously."

"Don't see how. You've done nothing but sit there watching us all night."

"It's no different from watching a football game."

"At least in football people get hit."

"The night's still young."

A full bellied laugh escaped Craig's mouth.

"You're right about that."

Gerald had not yet made eye contact with Craig. Craig followed Gerald's gaze to the dance floor where Anjelica was still tearing it up with her friends.

"You know...Anje's been looking forward to this dance forever. She started planning this night years before she met me. If I told her yesterday I was dumping her to marry her best friend who I got pregnant and we planned on going to prom together...Anje still woulda shown up tonight."

"Sounds about right."

Gerald lifted the plastic cup to his mouth and took a sip of punch.

"So you can understand how shocked I was when we got to prom and my girlfriend, who would rather cut off both of her legs than risk missing prom, suddenly decided that she couldn't bring herself to walk inside. Then, an even bigger shock, an hour later she walks in the door with you."

Gerald slowly rotated his head until Craig's glare encompassed his entire field of vision.

"You got somethin' you wanna say?"

"How close are you two? Really?"

Gerald could see Craig's muscles tensing up. He pondered the best way to handle this predicament. The wrong response would certainly lead to a physical confrontation. Gerald loved the idea of punching Craig in the face. He was sure he could win. Unfortunately, win or lose, if he punched Anjelica's prom date she would definitely be upset. This might be the one thing she couldn't forgive Gerald for.

"I love her. And to answer your next question, she loves me."

Wait. Don't roll your eyes. This is part of the plan.

"Can you understand why hearing that might not make me happy?"

Craig popped his neck then cracked his knuckles. Gerald calmly took a sip of his drink without ever breaking eye contact.

"Anje tells me you love your mom. That you love your dog. You love Peyton Manning. Have you ever wanted to stick your dick in any of them?"

Craig leaned back in his chair, still tense.

"I don't know whether to laugh or punch you."

"There are different kinds of love. The love she feels for me is different than the love she feels for you."

"And what about the love you feel for her."

Gerald took a deep breath. He'd rather not lie, but telling the truth would only do harm.

"It doesn't matter what I feel. Between the two of us, she'll always choose you."

"She chose you tonight."

Gerald shook his head.

"She knew I wasn't gonna say no to her. I know how much this means to her. I couldn't ruin her night."

"And you're so sure that next time she won't choose you."

Gerald stared silently at Craig.

"Say something."

"There's nothing I can say that'll ease your mind. Some things in life can't be proven. You just have to believe."

"Hey guys."

Gerald and Craig both tried to hide the shock on their faces when they turned their heads and saw Anjelica approaching the table with that familiar smile.

"What are you two talking about?"

"Sports."

"Yeah. Sports."

Anjelica sat in the chair next to Craig and draped her arm over his shoulders.

"Why'd you stop dancing?"

"I can't match your stamina. I need a break."

He leered over at Gerald.

"But Gerald's been sitting here all night. I'm sure he has plenty of energy."

"He's got a point Gerald."

Anjelica jumped to her feet and ran to the other side of the table. She grabbed Gerald's arm and playfully starting yanking him towards the dance floor.

"Come on. Come on."

Gerald shook his head."

"I don't dance."

"Yes you do. You've danced with me before."

"But I don't want to right now."

"Why not?"

Gerald briefly shot Craig a glance.

"I'm just not in a dancing mood."

"But we promised to dance together."

"I agreed to come. I never said anything about dancing."

"Yes you did. In seventh grade."

"What?"

"Remember? In seventh grade I promised to save you a dance. I wanna keep that promise."

Gerald couldn't help but smile. Anjelica was still that same toddler who saw a friendless boy sitting alone and decided she needed to help him. It was honestly a bit annoying. Gerald noticed the smile on Anjelica's face starting to fade. Well, he couldn't let that happen. Gerald smiled and said "ok." Anjelica's smile brightened and with one furious yank she pulled Gerald onto the dance floor.

Chapter 9
12th Grade

Anjelica wanted to do something special for Labor Day weekend. No clue why the idea popped into her head, but, she always wanted to have a real life picnic. She invited Craig, Gerald, Juan, Juan's boyfriend Garett and her friends Janice and Emma. Sunday afternoon they met at a park for what they thought would be a peaceful afternoon together.

Things were going wrong all day. People showed up late, the park was loud and crowded. The blistering heat had them drenched in sweat. They were surrounded by ants before they even finished setting up the blanket. A cloud of flies started licking their lips the moment they started pulling out food. They hurried through the meal and proceeded to vacate the park. As Juan helped Anjelica gather everything up Gerald stood off to the side staring at the sky.

"You plannin' to help?"

"Nope."

"Why the hell not?"

"Cause I don't feel like leavin'."

Gerald walked over to a large tree and lied in the grass under the shade of its leaves, the top of his head touching the trunk. Anjelica and Juan looked at each other, shrugged, then dropped everything and walked over to the tree. They lied down, sandwiching Gerald between them, and stared at the clouds for a few minutes before Juan broke the silence.

"You ever stop to think about the fact that we're not kids anymore? We're seniors. Soon we'll be graduating and heading into the real world."

"I try not to think about the future. It's too depressing."

"Ya hafta think about the future Gerald. It's almost here."

"Have you put any thought into the kind of career you want?"

"I haven't put any thought into what I wanna eat for dinner tonight."

"Have you thought about what you wanna do Juan?"

"Yeah. I think I'm gonna try for a law degree."

"Really? A lawyer? You?"

"Gerald!"

"What?"

"Why do you wanna be a lawyer?"

"I don't know. I just…I wanna make a difference. Change people's lives. Save some lives."

"That's sweet."

"Whadda you wanna do Anje?"

"I'm gonna be a doctor?"

"Like a surgeon?"

"God no. I've never been good with blood and guts. I figure I'll either be a pediatrician, cause I love kids, or an optometrist, cause that's the one where I'm least likely to pull something gross out of someone's body."

"What about you Gerald?"

Gerald shrugged.

"I've legitimately never thought about it."

"You need to. Tomorrow will be here sooner than you think."

"I'm not worried. It'll work out somehow."

The next morning Gerald arrived to school early so he could visit the guidance counselor. He paced back and forth in front of her desk.

"I'm freaking the fuck out."

"Calm down Gerald."

"Calm down? I never planned on graduating high school. Suddenly everyone expects me to have my entire life planned out? Why am I the only one who doesn't have his shit together?"

She took off her glasses and placed them on her desk. Then she let out a sigh and tilted her head, resting it on her fingertips.

"I can fix this very easily. But I need you to follow my instructions. Can you do that?"

"I'm desperate. I'll try anything."

She cleared her throat and pointed to the monochrome chair opposite her desk. An emotionally exhausted Gerald plopped his butt down on the cold plastic.

"Now take a deep breath in. The biggest one you can."

Gerald glared across the desk at her. She patiently stared back until he finally inhaled.

"Now stop, hold it."

Gerald held his breath for about three seconds.

"Let it out slowly."

As Gerald pushed a steady stream of air from his mouth he felt his body getting lighter.

"Feel better?"

"A little."

"Good. Now, do you want me to tell you why you haven't figured out your next move yet?"

"Because I suck."

She chuckled.

"Gerald, the truth is…nobody has everything figured out. We're all just guessing our way through life. Hell, I'm 33 with a full time job and I still don't know what I wanna be when I grow up."

Gerald rolled his eyes.

"It sure as hell feels like they got it figured out. It seems like everyone at this school has their entire futures mapped. Why don't I get a map? Where the hell is everyone finding theirs?"

"The only reason they know more than you is because they've thought about it more than you. You just said earlier that you didn't even plan on graduating high school. Well, some people have been planning to go to Harvard since they were four. High school is just a stone on the path for them."

"So you're saying I'm too late? I'm too far behind to catch up?"

"Not at all. I'm saying you don't have plans for your future because you never stopped to make those plans. The only way to know what you're doing tomorrow is to decide what you want to do tomorrow."

Gerald slumped further down until his butt nearly slid off the chair. He lifted his head to stare at the ceiling.

"I don't even know where to start."

"You start by closing your eyes."

Gerald looked back at her with his eyebrows raised.

"It's the easiest way to do this. Close your eyes and think of all the things in this world that make life worth living."

Gerald closed his eyes and visions of sugar plums began dancing in his head. Yeah right, I'm kidding. Obviously he thought of Anjelica. She was there for all the happiest moments of his life. It's because she was there that they were the happiest moments of his life. Watching her dance. Watching her smile. Hearing her laugh.

"I see that smile. What are you thinking of?"

Gerald's smile vanished instantly as his eyes flicked open.

"Nothing you can help me with."

"Try me."

Gerald lowered his head and mumbled to himself.

"I want the girl I like to love me back."

"Ouch. Sorry, but you're right. I can't help with that one."

"Know anyone who can?"

"Unfortunately, there might not be anything anyone can do about it. Sometimes the person you like just doesn't feel the same. It's painful. It hurts like hell. And the only thing you can do is just wait it out. Time is the only thing that fixes a broken heart."

"You asked me what made me happy. She's the only thing that came to mind."

"I was thinking more career wise. What kind of things do you like doing? Do you enjoy making anything? Food? Furniture? You'd be shocked what you can make a career out of. There are more choices than just the doctors and lawyers you see on TV."

Gerald stared at her, unable to open his mouth. There were plenty of things on his mind. He didn't feel like any of them were worth saying out loud.

"Gerald, take the next few days, maybe even a few weeks, however long you need. Just think long and hard about everything in life that you feel passionate about...other than your crush. You might be surprised at what you discover."

The rest of the day, Gerald didn't pay attention in any of his classes. He spent the entire morning completely zoned out, giving pre-programmed responses to every question he was asked. Next thing Gerald knew he was sitting at lunch with a tray of lukewarm cafeteria pizza in front of him.

For some strange reason his body started swaying. There was a pinching sensation on his arm. As his mind drifted back to reality he heard his name being whispered. As he began to fully regain consciousness the voice grew louder. He realized it was Anjelica. She was sitting to his left, gripping his arm and shaking him.

"Gerald. Gerald."

"Huh? What? What's wrong?"

"You tell me. You've been in the clouds all day. Everything alright?"

"Yeah. I'm fine."

"Come on. Talk to me."

She laid her hand on top of Gerald's. He tried to hide his smile, not wanting to show how much pleasure he drew not only from the warmth of her touch but the disdain on Craig's face.

"Tell me what's wrong. I might be able to help."

Gerald turned his hand up so he could grab hers.

"I guess yesterday's conversation bothered me more than I wanted to admit."

"Don't worry. Your grades are good enough you should be able to get accepted to some really good schools. Your life story will definitely make one hell of a college essay. And with your background there's gotta be some scholarship opportunities available."

"I'm not worried about any of that. What's the point of going to college at all if I don't have some sort of plan? I don't wanna waste years of my life and thousands of dollars when I don't have a clear purpose."

"Have you tried talking to the guidance counselor? Isn't helping kids figure this shit out the main point of her job?"

"I talked to her this morning. She told me you can make a career out of almost anything these days. That I should just take time to figure out what I love doing most and focus on a career where I do that thing. That's what I've been doing all day."

"Well, what have you thought of so far?"

He looked down at her hands, so small and soft. He gently caressed her fingers.

"I honestly can't think of anything."

Other than you. Just three more words he could never say to her.

"I'm sure you'll figure it out. I believe in you."

She pulled her hand away from his. It wasn't a violent jerk. Her fingers were like a feather tickling his palm. To Gerald, it felt like Scorpion flung a kunai into his chest and ripped his heart out. He sullenly stared at his fingers for a few seconds before returning to his meal.

When School ended Gerald went straight home He was shocked to enter his room and see Juan laying in his bunk with headphones on. Gerald grabbed a dirty t-shirt off the floor and playfully flung it at Juan's face. Juan tossed the shirt aside and took off his headphones.

"Sup?"

"Did you leave during lunch and decide not to go back?"

"I came straight home after my last class."

"Did you run here?"

"I don't have 7th or 8th period. You know that."

"I didn't know that. When did that happen? Are you allowed to just drop classes? Why was I never told this?"

"I never had any scheduled. Unlike some people I showed up to school every day for three years and passed every class. They ran out of classes to give me."

"See I know that's bullshit cause even when I half-assed it I never failed a class. Neither did Anje. You have free periods cause you chose not to sign up for any electives."

Gerald dropped his backpack and kicked off his shoes.

"If you have two free periods how do I always beat you home?"

"Cause I actually have a life."

"So your boyfriend was busy today and you couldn't think of anything to do."

"Basically."

As Gerald ascended the ladder Juan unplugged the headphones so Gerald could hear the music too. They both lied there silently. While Juan was letting the music wash over him Gerald couldn't relax his mind. Thoughts of the unknown future that lied ahead tortured him relentlessly.

"Hey Juan."

"Yeah?"

"Why'd you decide to be a lawyer?"

"I already told you. I wanna help people."

"I know, but…why'd you decide being a lawyer was the best way to do that?"

After a few seconds of silence Juan replied.

"Because of you."

After taking a few seconds to recover from the shock Gerald crawled over the edge of the bed to look down at Juan.

"What's it got to do with me?"

Juan rolled onto his side, facing the wall.

"When you were in the hospital, they kept telling us you were fine, but...I just wanted to see you, ya know. Verify for myself that you really were ok. There was all this red tape. They wouldn't let me in. Trying to adopt you was such a hassle. And soon as it was legal they threw a bunch of medical bills at us. Mom had to sue the cops just to save us from bankruptcy."

Juan's voice was cracking. Gerald could tell he was fighting back tears.

"The whole time we were going through all of this and I just couldn't stop thinking...if only there was some way I could help. Something I could do for her...for you...for me. It kinda just grew from there."

Gerald was dazed. A strong desire to help his mom and best friend led Juan to a career choice. Who knew you could build such a strong foundation for the future based off one simple thought? Gerald rolled onto his back and stared at the ceiling while a flood of memories surged through his mind.

His friendship with Anjelica began because a four year old made a split second decision to show kindness to a stranger. Life is defined by those fleeting moments. He's always hated chaos theory. There's nothing more frightening than the thought that your entire life is determined by that time when you were eight and chose a chicken salad sandwich instead of a tuna melt.

Juan turned up the volume on the speakers to drown out the deafening silence. It couldn't quiet the storm raging in Gerald's heart. He was in the middle of a fleeting moment.

12th Grade

The next decision he made could follow him for decades. He thought back to the various fleeting moments in his life. What choices did he make? Whenever Anjelica was involved the majority of Gerald's decisions were based entirely on what was best for her, regardless of the effect on him.

Gerald slid off his bunk, landing with barely a thud, and walked out of the room, pulling the door closed behind him. He meandered through the apartment until he found himself in the kitchen. There was plenty of food in the fridge but nothing he felt like eating. He settled for a soda and a bag of chips, then headed to the couch where he plopped down and watched TV.

He paid no attention to the passage of time. Just continued popping one chip in his mouth after another until the bag and can were empty. The front door swung open. Juan's mother entered with a dozen grocery bags hanging from each arm. She glanced at the crumb covered slob sinking deeper and deeper into the couch and sighed.

"Did you buy more chips?"

"It's getting harder to tell the two of you apart."

"I'm the one with darker skin."

She pushed the door closed with the heel of her foot then headed for the kitchen. Gerald stood up and walked her way, brushing a trail of crumbs onto the floor. Juan's mom shot him a stinging glare.

"I'll vacuum later. Promise."

As Gerald helped Juan's mom unload the groceries into the fridge and cupboards she noticed he was oddly silent.

Even when they met for the first time he wasn't this distant. She grabbed his arms and stared in his eyes.

"Ok. Tell me what's wrong."

"Whadda ya mean?"

"Something's clearly on your mind."

"Not really."

"Gerald, come on. You're obviously worried about something. You'll feel better if you talk about it."

Gerald leaned back against a counter and stared down at the can of soup in his hands.

"I was just wondering…why'd you adopt me?"

"Where's this coming from?"

"No reason. I just…I was just wondering."

"Well…I don't know what to say. It's not much of a mystery. I adopted you because Juan asked me to."

"That's all it took? He said please and you caved?"

She chuckled.

"Of course not. There were a handful of arguments. But, in the end, there was a kid in trouble and I was capable of helping him. It would be wrong not to. Plus, I knew Juan would never forgive me if I didn't."

The next morning Gerald showed up to school early to speak with the guidance counselor.

"It's a noble profession. I'm just curious how you came to this decision."

"Well, I have no marketable skills other than good memory, hard worker, and good listener. Now how does that translate to a job? Then I thought about my life? So much of it revolved around other people. I lived most of my life trying to make Anje happy, even if it cost my own. When my mom was beating me, I didn't hate her. I wanted to be a better son."

"That's actually very common among abuse victims."

"Don't you see? My natural tendency is towards helping others. That's how I got to psychologist. Then I thought about how expensive mental health is and how few people take it seriously. I won't be able to help the ones who need it most. And that's what I want. A job that helps those who need it most.

I remember how relieved I felt to finally get away from my mom. Living with Juan isn't perfect, but only when I found a home did I finally understand I'd never really had one before. That's when it hit me. I can be a social worker. Not everyone gets as lucky as me. They don't all have great friends who comes to their rescue. How many abuse victims turn runaway turn Jane Doe in the morgue? I can save lives."

"Do you mind if I give my opinion?"

Gerald threw his hands in the air.

"Oh come on. After all this time tryna get me to pick a career I finally choose one and you're gonna say I shouldn't?"

"My only advice is: choices made in the heat of emotion don't always turn out well."

Gerald placed his hands on his hips

"I know that. I know that, but, well...this is as good a place to start as any. I can always change my mind later. But I don't wanna start college with no sense of direction at all."

"Both solid points. So why don't we start looking for colleges that offer programs for social work."

Gerald plopped down in a chair.

"Stay local. Juan's mom can't afford to send one of us to a university, much less both. And we don't wanna spend the rest of our lives bogged down by crippling debt."

Gerald and Juan applied to every community college in the city. They applied for multiple grants and scholarships so tuition and books would be covered. Plus, staying local means they don't have to move out of mom's place. It's easy to save money when you're not paying rent or buying groceries. Juan's mom told them they'd have to learn to ride the bus. She wouldn't have time to drive them around.

Anjelica offered to give them both driving lessons. Neither of them saw the point, since it would be at least ten years before either of them could afford a car. Still, Gerald never turned down an opportunity to spend time with Anjelica. Speaking of Anjelica, she basically applied to every university in the country. She got accepted to….basically all of them. She could pick any school she wanted in any state she liked. It was her worst nightmare.

"The main reason I applied to so many schools is cause I expected the vast majority of them to turn me down. Now I have way too many choices and no idea how to start narrowing them all down."

Gerald was sitting on the couch in Anjelica's living room watching her pace back and forth in front of him. She said she had something important to discuss so he dropped everything and ran right over.

"Well, the easiest way to start is by eliminating the obvious bad choices."

"What bad choices? They're all great choices."

"Since you do have so many options you have to be as picky as possible. Any little inconvenience becomes an excuse. It's too expensive. Too far away. Too cold."

"But how expensive is too expensive? How cold is too cold? How far is too far?"

Anjelica dropped onto the cushion next to Gerald and rested her head on his shoulder. In that moment he felt the rest of the world melt away. He felt his heartbeat slowing down to match hers.

"Maybe you should just stay here."

Anjelica lifted her head to look at Gerald."

"Why?"

Gerald scrambled desperately for some believable excuse why it's better for her to stay when truthfully he just couldn't stand the thought of losing her. They had trouble staying in touch when they saw each other every day. If she moved to another state he might never see her again. No fate could be worse.

"Well…think about it."

He adjusted his position so his entire body pointed towards her.

"Life's gonna be changin' a lot next year. New school, new classes, new teachers, new friends. All those changes will be easier to face if you have friends and family with you. Your dad. Your friends. Craig…me."

Gerald stared at her nervously. His body was trembling and his breathing labored. Then, a gentle smile spread across Anjelica's face. She threw her arms around Gerald's neck and squeezed tight.

"Thank you."

With that, Anjelica's mind was set. She would be attending college in San Antonio. That way she saved money and preserved much of her daily life. Same city, same house. Many of the same friends. Unfortunately, there was one complication she didn't anticipate.

"I thought you got into Northeastern?"

Craig stood in front of Anjelica with a scowl he normally reserved for Gerald.

"I did get in. I decided I don't wanna move that far away."

"But we had a plan. We were gonna move in together. Help each other study."

"We can do all of that right here in this city."

"No we can't."

"Why the hell not?"

"Cause I didn't apply to a single college in this state."

Anjelica's jaw dropped. She had to take a step back.

"I thought we applied to all the same schools? Didn't we fill out those applications together?"

"Yeah I filled them out but I didn't mail any of 'em."

"Why the hell not?!?"

"Because unlike you I know exactly what I want to do with my life and exactly where I need to be to accomplish my goals. Boston has always been my priority."

"Then why bother filling them out at all?"

"That's what a boyfriend is supposed to do. He does things he doesn't want to do to make his girlfriend happy."

"So you never once stopped to consider the possibility that I would chose a college outside of Boston?"

"You hadn't even made up your mind yet. I figured it wouldn't be too hard to convince you."

"Seriously? You thought you could just go wherever you want and force me to follow you."

"Why not? You don't even know what you want."

"I know I don't want you."

Anjelica spent the next two weeks freezing Craig out. For the first couple of days Craig did nothing. He figured she'd calm down in a few days. That made things worse. Instead of apologizing he waited for her to crawl back to him.

"It's not even about college. It's the betrayal. Instead of telling me to my face how he felt he went behind my back and did whatever he wanted expecting me to follow his lead."

Gerald was sitting on the bottom bunk watching Anjelica pace back and forth in front of him. His heart was torn. As much as he hated seeing Anjelica in pain there was also a strong sense of relief…and hope. Hope that the door might be opening just a crack.

"I love the guy…I just can't stand him. He's so selfish and overbearing. Always tries to control my life. Tell me what friends I'm allowed to spend time with, what college to do to. You know how frustrating that is?"

Gerald knew exactly what he should say. He only hesitated because he was worried that he might be saying it for the wrong reason.

"Maybe you should take this as a sign."

She stopped in her tracks and whipped her head his way.

"Since when do you believe in fate?"

Gerald rubbed the back of his head.

"I don't. It's just that…lately…pretty much for the past year you can't mention his name without complaining about something. Maybe your physical distance is changing to match your emotional distance."

Anjelica's heart dropped to her toes. She dropped down next to Gerald on the bed.

"When exactly did you become a shrink?"

Gerald rotated his body towards her.

"I don't have all the answers Anje, but, I do have a few facts that are worth paying attention to. There are very few people who marry their high school sweetheart, long distance relationships rarely work and the odds decrease the younger the couple is. Maybe now is the best time to evaluate how hard you're willing to work to keep him in your life beyond high school."

Anjelica let out an exasperated sigh and fell back on the bed. She stared up at the bottom of the top bunk while pondering her feelings.

"I love him. I really do. No matter how much he frustrates me, no matter how much he tries to boss me around, control me…I've never not loved him."

"Just not enough to follow him to Boston."

Gerald gently laid a hand on top of Anjelica's while trying hard to keep his smile suppressed. This wasn't the time to gloat. The most important thing in that moment was to comfort his friend in her moment of pain. To be the shoulder she cried on. He'd wait until she left before he laughed and danced around the room.

"You know what you have to do."

She turned her hand up and clutched his.

"I know. But that doesn't make it any easier."

Anjelica squeezed Gerald's fingers as a tear rolled down her cheek. Gerald leaned over and kissed her forehead. His heart ached. Even though this was exactly what he wanted…nothing could ever hurt more than seeing Anjelica cry. The only thing he could do was hold her, be sympathetic, and play her favorite Fergie song.

The next morning Anjelica wasted no time seeking Craig out. After weeks without talking they were about to have their final talk. There was a lot of yelling, even more tears. Anjelica unloaded months of frustration in a few minutes. It was painful, but necessary.

It wasn't her original intention. She planned to calmly and politely explain that the two of them just weren't a good fit for each other long term. The relationship wasn't meant to last forever and it would be better to say goodbye now rather than dragging it on any longer. Truth is, if he had been more understanding she might not have been able to see it through.

She walked into the conversation with plenty of doubts. Then they started talking. Well, she started talking. He started arguing. It seemed like he had a rebuttal for every word she said. By the end of the conversation she was relieved. This guy couldn't let her express a single heartfelt opinion without undercutting her. She would definitely be better off without him.

Still, it was the end of a very long relationship. One that took up a huge chunk of her life. She dedicated so much time and energy to make it work. She gave him so much love and passion. It was hard to let go. That night she buried her face in a pillow and cried herself to sleep.

The next day she was sitting next to Gerald at lunch when she looked across the cafeteria and saw Craig. The smile on his face brought tears to her eyes. She didn't want Craig to see her like that so she jumped to her feet and ran out the door. Gerald ran after her. He found her in the hallway, her back against the lockers, her hands covering her tear-riddled face. Gerald wrapped his arms around her and squeezed her tight. She clutched his sides and cried her eyes out for a minute.

"I dumped him. Why am I crying while he laughs like nothing's wrong?"

Gerald shrugged.

"Girls are more sensitive."

Anjelica reached up and tugged on Gerald's shoulders. "Tell me the truth."

Gerald took a deep breath in and let out a huge sigh.

"Do you really wanna hear it? No matter how painful?"

Anjelica nodded.

"It means one of two things. Either he never loved you as much as you loved him, or, even more likely, he's just better at hiding his emotions than you are."

Anjelica sniffled.

"I really hope you're right."

Anjelica took a step back and started wiping her face. She sat on the floor with her back against the lockers, her head hung low. Gerald slid down beside her.

"Senior year was supposed to be fun and easy. God. Now I have to find a date for prom."

"Well...not exactly..."

Anjelica tilted her head up. Gerald rubbed the back of his neck.

"I mean...I know I'm not the greatest consolation prize, but..."

"I would love to."

Gerald stared at Anjelica. She stared back. He was shocked by the amount of determination he saw in her eyes. It made him wonder if she was saying yes for the right reasons. Maybe he shouldn't have asked.

"You didn't even let me ask."

Anjelica wrapped her arms around Gerald's neck and kissed his cheek.

"Thank you."

For the rest of the school year Anjelica chose to stay single. A lot of people say things like "I'm going to take a year to find myself" only to get a boyfriend a month later.

Anjelica stuck to her principles. She turned down every guy that asked. It wasn't easy. The second she dumped Craig every senior at the school, half of which were already in relationships, started vying for her affection.

Some of Anjelica's friends were trying to set her up with guys they thought were cute. It led to a few arguments. Anjelica wasn't interested in starting a new relationship at that point in her life. Not with so many changes on the horizon. She wasn't the hook up for a few months then move on like it never happened kind of girl. If she happened to meet someone who made her heart melt she wouldn't be able to fight it, but, she didn't feel like she needed to go on date after date to find someone worth spending time with. Not when she already had amazing friends like Gerald keeping her company.

If you went to high school you might be able to guess what happened next. Since Anjelica refused to go on dates rumors circulated that she had a boyfriend. Maybe a guy at a different school? Maybe her boyfriend already had a girlfriend? Some people find it impossible to believe that any girl could actually be happy when she's not romantically involved. Some people are pathetic idiots.

Anjelica spent more time with Gerald than anyone else. They hung out after school and on the weekends. They went to the mall, the movies and the park. They attended every party together. After a while people begun speculating that the two of them were dating. Anjelica didn't mind the rumor. She was happy that people stopped hitting on her. Gerald was more like a bodyguard than a boyfriend. Gerald was hoping the rumor might someday become reality. He nearly got his wish.

As prom approached Gerald decided, without and prompting, prodding, or goading, to put together an elaborate promposal. He always hated public spectacles, felt like they were gaudy and unnecessary, but knowing there was no risk of being rejected he felt that a little public embarrassment was a small price to pay to put a smile on Anjelica's face.

Are you wondering why I didn't describe the promposal? It's because I want you to use your imagination. Picture the most flamboyant and extravagant promposal you could ever dream of. Then double it. That's what Gerald did for Anjelica. Yeah, that's why I skipped over it. Definitely not because I couldn't think of anything.

Gerald and Anjelica arrived to the prom in a brand new dress and tuxedo, bought to complement each other. I'll let you decide who wore which. Per usual, Anjelica danced the night away. Gerald tried his best to keep up with her but ran out of energy a few songs in and retreated to the tables to rest for a couple of songs before rejoining her.

It would be easy to say it was the best night of Gerald's life. Honestly, every day for the past three months had been the best day of Gerald's life. Every second spent with Anjelica was always the best moment of his life. The night was going perfect. Then Gerald had to pee.

He went to the men's room and stood in front of the urinal letting it flow free. Suddenly, a hand grabbed the back of his head and shoved his face into the wall. When he turned to face his assailant he was greeted by a fist to his face followed by a foot to the gut. When he doubled over in pain a knee cap hit him in the face.

Gerald fell face first to the floor. As he pushed himself up he saw blood on the floor. He wiped his mouth then looked at his hand. It was covered in blood. He scanned the floor and saw he was surrounded by three pairs of shoes. He raised his head until he saw Craig's face.

"I always knew you were gonna steal my girl."

"You can't steal a person. That would be kidnapping."

Craig kicked Gerald's ribcage causing Gerald to lose his balance and face plant into the growing puddle of blood. Then Craig kicked Gerald three more times in the exact same spot. Gerald coughed up some blood.

"You're fucking pathetic."

Craig and his friends started walking away but Gerald called out to him.

"I didn't steal her. You treated her like shit. You took her for granted and she left. The one you should be beating up is yourself."

Craig ran over and kicked Gerald in the side of his head knocking him unconscious. When Gerald opened his eyes he was looking up at the ceiling. Out of the corner of his eye he saw Juan sitting in a chair against the wall.

"Where am I?"

Juan chuckled as he leaned forward.

"You're in the nurse's office. Someone found you on the bathroom floor covered in blood and piss."

"Thanks for the visual."

Gerald grunted as he raised his arm to rub his bruised and swollen face.

"Yeah, he really did a number on you."

"It hurt like hell."

Gerald relaxed and stared at the ceiling. It hurt just to breathe.

"What did you tell Anjelica?"

"He told me the truth."

When he heard her voice Gerald lifted his head and saw Anjelica leaning against the wall in the far corner. Gerald angrily jerked his head back to Juan who threw his hands in the air and shrugged.

"She got here before I did."

Anjelica walked over and sat on the bed, her hip grazing Gerald's. She laid her hand on his.

"I didn't fight back. I wanted to. I knew I could kick his ass. But hurting him wouldn't change anything. So I didn't throw a single punch."

"I know."

Anjelica wrapped her arms around Gerald. He winced in pain. She apologized but didn't loosen her grip.

"I'm so proud of you."

She kissed Gerald's cheek. He rubbed the back of her head. Juan smiled and walked out of the room, closing the door behind him. Gerald felt a surge of pain and reach for his ribs.

"Nothing broke. You lost a tooth and it cut the inside of your mouth. That's the only reason you were bleeding."

"Good to know."

Gerald stared at Anjelica. Her eyes were cloudy. She cried recently. He placed a hand on her cheek, using his thumb to rub her dimples.

"I'm sorry I ruined your senior prom."

Anjelica shook her head.

"It's our prom Gerald. And you didn't ruin anything. Craig tried to but it's not over yet."

"You don't wanna go out there with me. Not lookin' like this."

Anjelica grabbed Gerald's chin and turned his head left and right then left again.

"Well…there's a little bruising, but, other than that you seem just fine. If you're that worried about it though we can probably cover it up with some makeup."

"Makeup?"

"I don't have anything that naturally matches your shade but with some blending we can make it work."

"Guys don't wear makeup."

"Tell that to Ru Paul."

"Would you date Ru Paul?"

"In a heartbeat. The man is gorgeous."

"In that case, make me pretty."

"I've been wanting to do this for 14 years."

Anjelica ran out of the room, returning a minute later with an overstuffed purse. Using combinations of foundation, concealer and bronzer Anjelica worked her magic while Gerald sat patiently. It wasn't too difficult. He enjoyed the view. After nearly half an hour Anjelica took a step back to admire her masterpiece.

"Well, it's not perfect, but, 98% of your face is the same color. I can't do much about the swelling."

"Am I beautiful?"

"You're the prettiest one here."

"Second prettiest."

Anjelica jumped to her feet and held out her hands.

"Come on. We've got a dance to finish."

Gerald took Anjelica's hands and followed her back to the crowded ballroom. They definitely got a few looks. Neither of them cared very much. As they walked to the center of the dance floor the DJ got on the microphone.

"Alright everybody. It's been a fun night but all good things must come to an end. So grabs your partners and hit the floor for the last dance."

As an all too familiar guitar chord started playing Gerald took Anjelica into his arms. She wrapped her arms around his neck and they spent the next four minutes staring into each other's eyes as they gently swayed back and forth.

With her chest pressed against his Anjelica could feel his heart beat. The rhythm so gentle and soothing. She did too good a job with his makeup. Gerald looked really handsome. He was always caring and generous. So protective and reliable. She could see herself falling in love with a guy like him some day. Maybe she could even see herself falling in love with him.

That thought remained in her head after the music stopped. It was in the front of her mind as they sat beside each other on the ride home. It's the reason why, when the limo stopped in front of her house, Anjelica asked Gerald to walk her to the door. He had no reason to say no.

Gerald unbuckled, exited the limo, walked around to the other side and opened Anjelica's door. He held out his hand to her. She took it and followed him out of the car and he guided her up the walkway. Then they stood there, bathed in the glow of porchlight. Anjelica placed her hands on Gerald's shoulder, pushed herself up and wrapped her lips around his.

If it was Gerald's decision this tale would end right here. The perfect happily ever after. Unfortunately, as you can plainly see, we still have two more chapters. I'm sorry Gerald. I can't give you the happy ending you want. The story wouldn't be quite as meaningful.

Chapter 10

College

Sparks. Chemistry. Butterflies. Twitterpated. There are many different words and phrases used to describe the attraction one person feels towards another. Gerald spent more than half his life feeling those sparks. Before he knew what love was he knew he loved Anjelica. Senior prom was the greatest night of his life.

He spent the entire night with the woman he loved. He held her in his arms. They danced. Then, in that magic moment, she kissed him. It was the fairy tell ending he never dreamed would happen. If real life were like a move that's when the fireworks would've gone off. He'd get lifted into the air and magically transform into a handsome prince. Then a cheesy love song would play as the credits rolled.

If only Anjelica felt the same. That night she felt something for Gerald that he never once felt about her. Something she spent the majority of their relationship feeling about him. She felt comfortable. Her heart didn't flutter. Her tongue wasn't tied. Her stomach wasn't in knots.

As she stood there in his arms, every urge and musing that had been coursing through her body dissipated the instant their lips touched. She didn't hate the kiss. She definitely didn't hate Gerald. She wasn't disgusted. She just wasn't excited. It was the most boring kiss she'd ever had in her life.

Kissing Gerald's lips basically elicited the same emotional response as kissing her dad on the cheek. Or kissing the dog. Yeah, that was it. Gerald was less like a boy to Anjelica and more like a pet. He was fiercely loyal and protective. No matter how far they drifted from each other he always found his way back to her.

Sadly, it all came down to timing. If they met for the first time when Anjelica was a forty year old divorced mother of two Gerald is exactly the guy she would fall for. Alas, they were only teenagers. When you're that young every decision in your life is usually guided almost entirely by that spark…or lack thereof.

Though they hid it well, the next few weeks were a bit awkward for both of them. Anjelica was afraid to mention the kiss. As much as she wanted to talk about it she couldn't stand the thought of Gerald hating her again. So she stayed quiet, hoping he'd never bring it up. Thankfully, Gerald was so afraid of pushing things too much and potentially scaring her away that he said nothing as well.

Graduation came and went. The summer somehow managed to pass even faster. Gerald managed to hold onto hope for as long as he could but college was starting and Anjelica still gave no indication that the kiss was anything more than an empty gesture. Whether she was swept away in the moment or just felt like it was a necessary part of the social contract, the kiss clearly meant less to Anjelica than it did to Gerald.

Gerald dove headfirst into school, taking as many classes as he was allowed, hoping to transfer to UTSA as soon as possible so his life could be more like high school again, back when he actually got to see Anjelica every day. They still texted every day, constantly messaged on social media, but it wasn't the same as sitting next to each other at lunch.

Gerald and Juan still lived together so despite going to different schools they spent enough time together to get on each other's nerves. Gerald took a part time job at a temp agency. Though they offered him plenty of assignments he turned down more than he accepted. He liked extra money but he didn't actually need it. His main focuses in life were school...and Anjelica.

Anjelica was a full time college student with a full time job who never had trouble making friends with basically every human she encountered. Before classes began she promised Gerald they'd spend every weekend together. That promised lasted almost through the end of September. Between classes, homework, her new friends and the new job Anjelica barely had time to sleep, shower and eat.

To make matters worse, on her very first day of classes Anjelica met a boy named Kyle. A nearly six feet tall peach skinned boy with a mop top that flopped down to his shoulders and that cocky smile that every teen heartthrob had in the 90s. He was a pencil thin, with well-toned muscles, former high school soccer star now struggling to find playing time on the college team. That one simple fact greatly eased Gerald's mind. He appreciated anything negative that could be said about that guy.

Kyle definitely wasn't rich but his family never struggled. He never once wondered where his next meal would come from. Like everyone he had his own struggles in life. It's not like he always got everything he wanted. However, he did get the one thing Gerald always wanted.

After they'd been dating for a while Kyle made a confession to Anjelica. The first time they bumped into each other was an accident. Every time after that was him going out of his way to put himself in her path. A little creepy? Yes. Should this behavior be encouraged? No. The problem is, Kyle is really cute. So instead of being weirded out Anjelica found it charming.

The first time Gerald met Kyle was on Thanksgiving. Anjelica invited her closest friends to her place. Gerald showed up with Juan, Juan's boyfriend, and Juan's mom. When Kyle arrived Anjelica introduced him as her new boyfriend. He made a great first impression. They could understand why Anjelica fell for him. Hell, Gerald might've fallen for the guy if he wasn't so insanely jealous.

Kyle was easily the sweetest boyfriend Anjelica ever had. Everyone was rooting for them. Kyle was a great guy and they loved the idea of him sticking around for a long time. Gerald was the only one hoping they'd break up. Well, unless this is the first chapter you're reading you should know by now that Gerald rarely gets what he wants. Kyle and Anjelica spent thanksgiving, Christmas and New Year's together. Then Valentine's Day. Then spring break. When summer came around they spent every waking moment together. Every sleeping moment as well.

When they celebrated the one year anniversary of the day they met it was clear to everyone that this could be the one that last forever. After a year and a half of dating Kyle asked Anjelica to move in with him. Over the summer they found a small apartment together that they could call home.

When her junior year started Anjelica was the happiest human on the planet. She was living with her amazing boyfriend. Her best friend Gerald transferred to her school making it much easier for them to spend time together. She legitimately could not imagine her life being any better.

Then came that cold day in the third of November. Gerald was working at a retail store. He'd been making regular appearances there. They were considering making him a full time employee. Halfway through the shift Gerald got a phone call. Normally he left his phone in the back when he worked. If he kept it on his person he'd turn it off, or at least silence it. That day he did neither.

When his phone started ringing he only pulled it out so he could turn it off. Then he saw it was Anjelica and something inside him knew he had to answer. When he heard her sobbing voice Gerald didn't hesitate to run out the door. It might've cost him his job but when Anjelica was involved nothing else mattered.

Anjelica was at her father's house. Gerald arrived to find her sitting on her bed, leaning up against the headboard clutching a tear-soaked pillow. He couldn't think of anything worth saying. He simply sat beside her and draped his arm over her shoulders. She leaned over and cried into his chest for half an hour.

When her tears dried she laid there in silence for about twenty minutes before explaining everything to Gerald. On Halloween Anjelica and Kyle went to a costume party together. They got separated and she didn't see him for a few hours. When she was ready to go home she went looking for him. She found him. After wondering around the house, peeking in every room she passed, she opened a bedroom door to see him having sex with some other girl.

She couldn't believe what she saw. She didn't want to believe it. This is the man she was planning to marry. She never knew it was possible to feel so much pain. She hadn't seen him since. She went straight to her dad's place and only left her room to pee. Kyle stopped by once and Humberto nearly stabbed him with a screwdriver.

Anjelica didn't know what to do next. They moved in together. They were planning their future. Gerald was confused himself. He hated seeing Anjelica sad. Every tear that fell from her eyes was like a bullet hitting is heart. At the same time, he was fighting with all his might to hold back a smile.

He hated seeing her cry but loved knowing that he was the first person she turned to for comfort. He's the shoulder she wanted to cry on and he was more than willing to carry all her burdens. He could feel in his heart that their close friendship was one short step away from romantic. Kyle may have pushed Anjelica further into Gerald's arms.

"Do you mind just holding me for a while?"

"Of course."

Anjelica wrapped her arms around Gerald's waist, rested her head on his chest and let the sound of his breathing soothe her to sleep. Gerald lost track of time. He just sat there staring at her, holding her steady while wondering how she could be so beautiful with a face covered in tears and snot. The moment she started snoring Gerald gently leaned her back, resting her head on the pillow. He pulled the covers over her and gave a gentle peck on her forehead before walking out of the room.

Gerald could've held her all night. He wanted to. Moreover, he wanted Anjelica to fall in love with him. He wanted their love to last forever. How many women marry their rebound? Maybe now would be a great time to put some distance between them. As much as Gerald hated the idea of emotional manipulation he'd seen it work. When she needed him most, force her to chase after him for once. As Gerald approached the front door Humberto approached Gerald.

"How's she doing?"

"Not well."

"Is she gonna be okay?"

Gerald shrugged.

"Only time will tell."

Humberto nodded then then reached out and gripped Gerald's shoulder.

"Thanks for always being there for her. She's lucky to have a friend like you."

With those words, all ambitions of using this moment of weakness to steal Anjelica's heart fled from Gerald's mind. If she needed him, he would be there.

"You have a goodnight sir."

"You too. Take care of yourself."

"I will."

Gerald patted Humberto on the back then walked out the door. Humberto locked the door behind him. As Gerald stepped off the curb he was flooded by light. He turned his head to see a car creep up, stopping just inches in front of him. The lights turned off and Kyle leaned out of the driver's side window.

"You need a lift?"

Gerald weighed his options for a second.

"Not really?"

"Get in anyways."

For the record kids, it's never a good idea to get into someone's car when they're being that aggressive. It can only lead to trouble. Unfortunately, Gerald had his own motives at that moment. He jumped into the passenger seat and they had a very tense conversation as they drove around the city. The words weren't vindictive, but there was a feeling of resentment in the air coming from both parties.

"How's Anje doing?"

"You actually care?"

"You tryin' to imply I don't?"

"If I am? You gonna push me out without stoppin'?"

Kyle gritted his teeth and for the next twenty minutes they endured a staunch silence.

"You know...I really have no idea where you live."

"Yeah. I figured that out 15 minutes ago."

"You weren't gonna say nothin'?"

"We were playing the quiet game. First one to talk loses."

"You serious?"

"I'm very competitive."

Kyle couldn't stop himself from chuckling.

"God you're amazing. I think that's the first time I've laughed since..."

"Halloween."

In an instant Gerald saw every ounce of joy erased from Kyle's body. He pulled over to the side of the road and put the car in park. He exhaled a heavy breath as he leaned back.

"How do I fix this?"

Gerald leaned forward, resting his forearms on the dashboard.

"You want an honest answer?"

Kyle nodded.

"No matter how much it might hurt to hear?"

Tears started welling up in Kyle's eyes.

"Please. I need to know."

Gerald took a deep breath.

"Ok. The truth is...you might not be able to fix it."

Some of you might have guessed that Gerald said this to permanently rid himself of this nuisance. You have every right to leap to that conclusion. However, you guessed wrong. Based on what he experienced earlier, Gerald honestly believed the words he said. Anjelica was acting like the relationship already ended.

"There's got to be a way."

Gerald turned his head and saw tears streaming down Kyle's face.

"Why'd you do it?"

Kyle wiped the tears from his face.

"I...I don't know."

Kyle swallowed a lump in his throat.

"I don't know. I really don't. I was drunk. She was hot. Heh, I thought I'd get away with it."

Careful Kyle. Gerald was one wrong word away from throwing punches.

"It was stupid. I never should've done it. But I did. And I've spent every second since regretting it."

Kyle turned to face Gerald with the eyes of a child that just saw a monster under his bed and ran out of his room searching for mommy.

"Tell me what I can do. I don't care what it is. I'll do anything. Just give me some sort of hope."

Gerald turned away from Kyle, staring out the window at the city lights.

"I'm sorry Kyle. You can't undo what you did. There's no taking it back."

Gerald paused as he thought on the words that were about to leave his mouth. Words that could alter many people's lives forever. He nearly chocked on them.

"Your relationship is over. She's already moved on. You should to."

Kyle's breathing got heavy. He repeatedly smacked the steering wheel with an open hand. He punched the dashboard, followed by head-butting the top of the steering wheel and kicking the door. Then he gripped the steering wheel with both hands and shouted violently at the top of his lungs.

Gerald could do nothing but sit there watching as the destruction he wrought unfolded. He thought being rid of Kyle would bring untold amounts of joy. Instead he felt nothing but guilt. Kyle rested his arms on the steering wheel then buried his face in them and cried.

"I can't accept that. Not until I hear her say it. Not until she looks me in the eyes and tells me she doesn't love me anymore."

While Kyle cried into his arms Gerald sat there staring at him silently. A million thoughts raced through his head. Gerald did nothing wrong. Kyle screwed up the relationship all on his own. Gerald simply did the smart thing and stayed out of the way, let nature take its course.

The next morning Anjelica was confused when she woke up and wasn't still in Gerald's arms. Even more shocked when she looked at the time and realized it was already well into the afternoon. She fully intended to lay back down, close her eyes and sleep for another three days. That is, until a familiar aroma wafted into the room.

With what little strength she had in her body Anjelica managed to pull herself out of bed and trudge down the stairs to the dining room where her father and Gerald were wearing aprons and setting the table. Her confusion, joy and every other emotion she felt were all suppressed by the hunger ravaging her body.

"Your dad says you haven't eaten since you came back. And this is usually the time you get up, walk to the bathroom, then head back to sleep. I figured you could use a good meal to give you energy for your next nap."

Anjelica gave Gerald a long hug. Then they sat down and ate their meal. Anjelica cleared most of the dishes herself. She was on her third course before Gerald finished his first. When the food was all gone Humberto volunteered to do the cleaning while Gerald and Anjelica sat on the couch watching TV.

"Are you ever going back to school?"

"Yeah. Next week. Dad told them I was in the hospital."

"What about Kyle? Is that really done for good?"

"Obviously."

"So where ya gonna live?"

"Well, it looks like I'm moving back here for a while."

"What about all your stuff?"

"I don't know. I guess I'll have to sneak over and steal it while Kyle's at work or something."

Anjelica pondered silently for a few seconds.

"Saturday. He works at a restaurant. Saturday is their busiest day. For as long he's had that job he's never taken a Saturday night off."

"Tomorrow's Saturday."

Anjelica smiled at Gerald. The next night she drove the two of them over to her place. She opened the door and nearly jumped out of her skin, also letting out a small shriek, when she turned on the lights and saw Kyle sitting on the couch.

"What are you doing here? Why aren't you at work? And why are you sitting in the dark?"

When the door slammed behind her Anjelica whipped her head around and saw Gerald locking it. She ran over to him and shoved him into a wall.

"You bastard! You knew he'd be here!?!"

"I texted him last night asking him to take the night off."

"Why? Why would you do this to me? You know I don't wanna see him!"

"If there's any chance of you two working this out you need to talk to him. And if there's no chance of things working out, you need closure. Either way, you two need to talk to each other. He needs to be here right now."

Anjelica's eyes welled up. Gerald felt so much guilt he couldn't bear to look at her. He turned his head away. Anjelica couldn't say a word. For all the anger she felt she also knew he was right. She just didn't want to face him because it was too painful. Sometimes in life the most important things are the ones that cause the most tears.

She turned to Kyle. His heart melted when he saw the tears streaming down her face. There were so many things he wanted to say. He practiced his apology so many times in the mirror. Standing there, looking in those eyes…he knew his words meant nothing right now.

"Kyle…It's over."

Tears started rolling down Kyle's face.

"Do you really mean that?"

Anjelica folded her arms across her chest.

"I do."

She was clearly forcing the words out. It made no difference. No matter the conviction behind them the words were said. Kyle took steps towards Anjelica, standing so close to her that their noses touched. She felt his heart racing. Her convictions wavered.

"Look me in the eyes and tell me you don't love me."

Anjelica swallowed a lump in her throat.

"I don't love you."

When those words left her mouth Kyle's soul shattered. In his heart he knew she was lying, but the fact that she was willing to say it proved how angry she was. Fighting would be futile. He walked back to the bedroom. Anjelica broke down in tears. She didn't believe the words she just said. She was just trying to end the conversation.

The moment she said it pain surged through her entire body, all the way down to her bones. It was like she got thrown into an iron maiden. Every inch of her body was being pierced by spikes. She was slowly losing what little strength she had in her body. Just before her legs gave out Kyle walked out of the bedroom with a suitcase.

"I've paid the next two month's rent. You can stay here."

Kyle walked past Anjelica and neither of them turned their heads. As Kyle unlocked the door Gerald couldn't stop staring at him. He was wondering how good a job he was doing containing his emotions. Could either of them see it on his face?

Could Kyle see how angry Gerald was about the pain Anjelica was in? Could Anjelica see the relief that Gerald felt about how things turned out today? How happy Gerald was to finally be free of the obstruction? No. Kyle couldn't see any of that. He was so wrapped up in his own feelings he barely even remembered Gerald was there.

The moment Kyle shut the door Anjelica crumpled to the floor and wailed like a baby. Gerald got on his knees, wrapped his arms around Anjelica and held her tight. Anjelica spent the rest of the weekend crying into Gerald's arms. Then Monday morning she showered, got dressed, then she and Gerald grabbed some breakfast together.

Anjelica went to classes, talked to friends, checked in at work and got her new schedule. She tried her best to get life back to normal, as if the past week just didn't happen. The sun went down and she got lonely. So she called Gerald.

"I just...I really don't wanna be alone tonight."

So Gerald went over and, for the third night in a row, he and Anjelica fell asleep in each other's arms. For the third morning in a row, they woke up still holding each other. Gerald could see all of his dreams coming true right before his eyes. Two more nights, two more mornings. Then one day Anjelica gave Gerald a gift.

It was a small box, fit perfectly in the palm of his hand, wrapped in a little red bow. From the size of it there were only so many things it could be. Gerald was going over the options in his head, trying to guess what Anjelica could possibly be thinking. The female mind is a landscape he's never been able to properly map. He lifted the lid and there was a small piece of metal.

"It's a key."

"I see that. What's it for?"

"For here."

"Here? What do you mean here?"

"I mean right here Gerald. The apartment."

"This apartment?"

"Yes."

"But…why?"

"Because I want you to move in with me."

"But…why?"

"Mostly because I can't afford this place on my own and I don't wanna move back home. And of all my friends, you're the one I trust most. I know you definitely won't fuck my boyfriend."

Gerald was equally ecstatic and insulted. Of course he would love living with Anjelica. However, the fact that she could ask so casually, not to mention the reason why she asked, deeply wounded his pride.

"This is a one bedroom. Where would I sleep?"

"We can buy a pullout couch."

"You can't afford rent but you can afford a new couch?"

We can save money to trade in for a used one. We bought this couch new. It's only lightly used. We never ate or had sex on it. The scotch guarding never wore out. We should still be able to get a good value for it."

"You're not worried I'll sneak into your room and rape you in your sleep?"

"Just try not to wake me up."

Gerald chuckled to hide the pain. Anjelica trusted her best friend would never do anything bad to her. In Gerald's eyes, it felt like Anjelica didn't see him as a man.

"I'll put a lock on the door if it makes you more comfortable."

She threw her arms around his stomach and rested her head on his chest.

"Come on Gerald. Please."

She knew exactly what she was doing. Don't pretend for a second that you actually think this wasn't on purpose. She fully understood the power she held over him. The combination of physical touch with a soft voice were a calculated move to break down Gerald's final barrier. He was now hopelessly wrapped around her finger.

"Sure. Why not?"

Gerald never told her, never told anyone actually, that he had a decent savings built. Juan's mom had a rule: as long as the boys were in school they didn't have to pitch in. The moment they dropped out, flunked out, or graduated they start paying rent and buying their own groceries. For the past two years Gerald saved every penny possible.

For the next month Gerald and Anjelica slept under the same roof. When two people cohabitate it's never without issue. Still, even when they were fighting Gerald couldn't stop smiling. Other than sleeping in separate rooms they felt like and old married couple.

A week into December the two of them were decorating the apartment. Green and red paper chain taped to the walls. A one foot tall Christmas tree adorned with balls, lights and tinsel. The show stopper was somewhat out of sight. Most people wouldn't see it if they weren't explicitly looking. A mistletoe taped above the door frame leading into Anjelica's bedroom.

"Why put it in the one place no one ever goes?"

"The only reason there aren't a ton of men constantly coming in and out of that room is cause I'm considerate of my roommate. I've had plenty of offers."

Gerald was amazed. Every word she said equally made his day and broke his heart. They each spent Christmas Eve at their respective homes. They woke up late, opened presents while watching Christmas movies, then ate a huge meal with their families before returning to their shared apartment. When Anjelica stepped through the door after sundown Gerald was already taking down the Christmas decorations.

"When did you become that guy?"

"What guy?"

"The one who loses all his Christmas spirit the moment he's done opening presents."

"I never had any Christmas spirit."

"Bullshit. All month you've been filled with Christmas spirit. You put up decorations, watched movies, listened to holiday tunes while we sipped eggnog."

"Just cause I did it don't mean I enjoyed it."

"Well why'd you do it if you don't like it?"

"Cause I wanted to."

"You just said you didn't want to."

"I said I didn't enjoy it. That's not the same as not wanting to."

"Why would you wanna do something knowing you don't enjoy it?"

"Because you wanted to."

For some reason she didn't understand Anjelica felt her heart skip a beat.

"Really? Is that all there is to it?"

Gerald nodded.

"That's what friends are for."

"No. No it's not. Juan is your best friend in the world. How often do you go this far out of your way for him?"

"Juan's not my best friend, he's my brother. You're my best friend."

Anjelica walked over to Gerald and grabbed his wrist.

"Is that really all I am to you?"

Her voice, like the sweet whispers of an angel, syphoned all the energy from Gerald's body. He wanted to cry. Tears of joy for being blessed to have someone so amazing in his life. Tears of pain from knowing she'd never feel the same way about him. He turned his head the other way.

"Gerald....look at me."

When he turned back to her she had a finger pointed up. He tilted his head and saw the mistletoe. He was so distracted by their conversation he hadn't even noticed he'd pulled all the paper chain off the wall from the front door to the bedroom. He looked back at her with uncertainty.

"You're always there for me. I can't count how many times you gave up your life to help me live mine. You are, without a doubt, the sweetest, most caring, thoughtful, compassionate man I've ever known."

She reached her arms up, wrapping them around his neck and pulling herself close. Her crotch pressed against his. Their stomachs pushed back and forth against each other as they breathed in and out almost in synchronous rhythm. Her chest pressed against his. She could feel his heart beating out of control.

Gerald's mind was being torn apart by warring emotions. He wanted to vomit, cry, laugh, leap for joy, shout at the top of his lungs and, most importantly, slap himself silly just to be sure he wasn't dreaming. No. It couldn't be a dream. Even in his wildest imagination he could never picture a scene like this.

"I'm so lucky to have you in my life. Sometimes I take you for granted. And, I guess...all this time I've just been scared that if things ever went wrong I'd lose my best friend. But I was wrong. I could never lose you. You and I were meant to be together forever."

She kissed him. It was the greatest Christmas present Gerald ever received. In that moment his entire life flashed before his eyes. All the pain he endured, all the heartache he felt, it was all worth it. A lifetime of pain melted away the moment she took him into her arms and declared they were forever.

Wouldn't it be nice if the story could end right here? I wish it could. Gerald deserves a perfect happily ever after. I bet some of you might look at how many sentences are left in this chapter and hope it's entirely about how Gerald and Anjelica's relationship continued to grow year after year. I'm sorry to disappoint you. Gerald finding happiness was never the point of this story.

At least he had some small taste of that perfect life he always dreamed of. For the next five weeks he and Anjelica were having wet and wild sex every night. They never fought, hardly ever disagreed about anything. Gerald couldn't imagine his life being anything better than that. It was the true definition of serenity.

Then, in a single instant, it all came crashing down. A moment before it happened Gerald could never have predicted how much that single second, that single word, could bring his entire existence crashing down. On the first day of February, while in the midst of a passionate romp, Anjelica shouted Kyle's name.

Everything came to a screeching halt after that. Not just for the night. For the next three days the apartment was Antarctica. Anjelica wanted to apologize but she was worried Gerald wouldn't accept it. Gerald would've loved to just pretend it didn't happened but every time he saw her his mind flashed back to that night. One day Gerald was washing dishes when Anjelica finally broke the silence.

"I'm sorry."

Really Anjelica? That's it? It took you three days to come up with that?

"I haven't heard from him since we broke up. He blocked me everywhere. None of his friends will tell me anything. All of my friends tell me to forget about him and move on."

"So why can't you?"

He turned around and glared at her. When she saw that look in his eyes she felt guilt and fear. She recognized that mix of anger and sadness. The last time she saw it was in seventh grade.

"We dated for two years. We lived together. I was in love with him. You don't just lose a bond like that overnight. If you lost someone you loved can you say for sure they'd never cross your mind again for the rest of your life?"

Gerald turned away.

"I just wanna know he's ok."

Gerald couldn't argue with her. Even if she dropped him like a rock Anjelica would still cross Gerald's mind from time to time, even years after he moved on. Strike that. She would never be absent from his mind. He would never move on.

Gerald forgave Anjelica and they had great makeup sex. Life returned to normal…save for one thing. Gerald saw a sadness forever looming in Anjelica's eyes. She hid it well. Her lips never said it. Her hips never showed it. Her breath never carried it. Still, Gerald saw it in her eyes. She was still worried about Kyle.

Gerald decided to do some investigating. It was a short inquiry. He started by asking Kyle's best friend Fred. Turns out, when Kyle moved out he showed up at Fred's door. Been there ever since. The next morning Gerald went to Fred's house. What awaited him was a hallowed out husk.

In the months after the breakup Kyle slowly fell into disarray. At first he was smiling and laughing like nothing was wrong. Still went to classes and work. As time went on his health and demeanor continually degraded. He stopped working out. He barely ate anything. Since the New Year began he had exactly one shower. Most importantly, he hadn't smiled in two months.

Gerald walked into the spare room where Kyle made his nest. The smell of liquor and vomit dominated his nostrils the moment he swung the door open. Kyle was passed out face down on top of the covers. The entire room was a mess. Clothes and crumbs scattered around. Gerald wouldn't be shocked if he lifted the bed and found and intrusion of cockroaches. Yes, a group of cockroaches is called an intrusion.

Gerald tiptoed through the roughage as he traversed the vast wasteland between the doorway and the bed. Upon reaching the bed Gerald gingerly sat down next to the motionless shell that used to be Kyle. Gerald nudged Kyle to see if he'd respond. The body was still warm. There was a slight groan. Gerald nudged again.

"Wakey. Wakey."

Kyle responded but his voice was muffled by a mouthful of pillow. Gerald nudged again and got the same muffled moans. Realizing his efforts were fruitless Gerald adjusted his approach. He stood up, grabbed Kyle's arm and started pulling.

Kyle offered no resistance, save but gravity, as Gerald dragged him off the bed, across the carpeted floor and onto the cold bathroom tiles. Gerald tossed Kyle's limp, listless body into the tub. Kyle squirmed around for a few seconds then comfortably fell asleep. Gerald made sure the showerhead was open, pointed it towards Kyle's face and turned on the cold water.

The water stirred Kyle from his sleep but he could barely muster enough strength to lift his arms in front of his face. When Gerald lowered the water pressure to a trickle Kyle spat out a mouthful of water and coughed a few times.

"The hell are you doing?"

"Wakin' you up."

Gerald turned the water back on.

"Hey! Stop!"

After much squirming Kyle managed to roll over, push himself onto his knees and start crawling out of the tub. Gerald turned the water off.

"The fuck are you doing here Gerald?"

"Came to check on you. See how you're doin'. Apparently not well. "

"How would you be if the love of your life dumped you?"

"Honestly, I'd probly try to kill myself. But I'd do it quick. Hang myself, OD, maybe a shotgun to the face. Definitely wouldn't go for liver damage. That could take a couple decades."

Kyle turned around and sat on the floor of the tub with his back against the wall. He looked up and saw Gerald holding a towel out to him. He grabbed it and dried his face.

"Look at you getting all scruffy. It's so cute when a boy tries to grow his first beard. Always so patchy."

"The fuck do you want?"

"I want you to shower, shave, brush your teeth, put on some clean clothes, clean your room, eat a nice healthy breakfast then spend the day hanging out with me."

Kyle shook his head.

"Too many instructions. I can do one, max two of those things. Three tops."

"Fair enough. Then start by showering and getting dressed."

Gerald turned the water back on. Kyle glared at him. Gerald chuckled as he walked out of the room, closing the door behind him. He headed to the living room where Fred was hitting from the bong while watching a morning talk show on TV.

"You guys got any food in the fridge?"

"We got hot pockets and sushi."

"Is the sushi from a gas station?"

"Does it matter?"

"At least tell me it's fresh."

"Your guess is as good as mine."

Gerald went to the kitchen, grabbed some hot pockets from the freezer and popped them in the microwave. Just as they finished a naked Kyle stumbled into the kitchen dripping wet.

"We're out of clean towels."

"That was quick. Did you even use soap?"

"We're guys. Rinse, soap, rinse. Only takes a minute."

"You'll have to forgive him Fred. He spent most of his life with women."

"Such a shame."

Gerald rolled his eyes and handed Kyle the plate. Then he walked to the bedroom and started rooting around in the mess looking for the least putrid articles of clothing. There were very few things that weren't dreadfully rank. He managed to find a suitable outfit and walked back to the kitchen where he tossed the clothes at Kyle.

"Cover that thing up before you poke someone's eye out. I'll be waiting outside."

Gerald walked outside and sat on the hood of Kyle's car. He waited patiently, partly hoping that Kyle decided to crawl back in bed. He was relieved and frustrate when Kyle walked out the front door.

"You got the keys?"

Kyle patted himself down then walked back inside. A minute and a half later he walked back outside with the keys in his hand. As Kyle got close to the car Gerald held out his hand.

"What?"

"Gimme the keys."

"Do you have a license?"

"I know how to drive."

"That's not what I asked."

"Don't worry. The cops won't pull me over if I got a white guy with me."

Kyle hesitated for a second before dropping the keys in Gerald's hand. They sat in silence for the majority of the ride, only the occasional cough or snort cutting through the awkwardness. When Gerald pulled the car into a packed parking lot Kyle peered through the window. There was a Ferris wheel, a carousel, food stalls and game booths.

"What is this?"

"I believe the technical term for it is a traveling funfair."

Gerald put the car in park and pulled the keys out.

"Why are we here?"

"The main objective is to have some fun."

Gerald hopped out of the car, slamming the door shut behind him. Kyle sunk deeper into his seat. Gerald walked to the passenger side and yanked Kyle out.

"You can't force someone to have fun. That's not how happiness works."

"Can't hurt to try."

Gerald spent the day dragging Kyle around from stall to stall, ride to ride. They ate cotton candy and corn dogs, played games and won prizes. Gerald had Kyle walking around with a monocle, a baseball cap and a large stuffed frog. When Gerald rode the carousel he drug Kyle along with him. As the horses circled Gerald looked over at Kyle, leaning against the pole with droopy eyes and an even droopier frown.

Gerald didn't have to ask what was wrong. He knew he wasn't handling the situation correctly, but he wanted to keep Anjelica all to himself. When the ride ended Kyle stumbled over to the nearest trash can and doubled over. As he vomited into the can he dropped his frog and monocle into the vomit filled receptacle.

"Dam. I'm glad there aren't any roller coasters here."

"Kyle sat down on the ground next to the trash can, clumps of vomit still dropping from his lips, one hand still dangling limp over the edge of the can.

"Why are you doing this to me?"

"It's been three months Kyle. That's a long time to spend wallowing."

"What else am I supposed to do? The love of my life dumped me. You can't expect me to just get over it."

Gerald bit the inside of his cheek.

"She did."

Kyle looked up, eyes wide with shock and anger. He used the trash can to push himself back onto his feet.

"What did you just say?"

Gerald licked his lips and turned his head away.

"She started seeing someone. Shortly after Christmas."

Kyle's stomach was doing summersaults. His heart was ready to explode. He kicked over the trash can. Then picked it up and slammed it down on the ground. Then kicked it one more time before falling to his knees and shouting at the sky. Then he fell to the ground, curled up in a ball and started crying.

"How can she move on so quickly? I thought she loved me?"

"She thought you loved her. You jumped in bed with someone else."

"I made a mistake! I fucked up! And I've regretted it every single second since. I would do anything to take it back. Anything!"

Gerald stood there staring at him, unsure of what to do. Part of him wanted to give Kyle a hug. Part of him wanted to walk away, pretend he didn't know Kyle and didn't see any of this. People were staring. Gerald knew nothing he said could ease Kyle's pain. He just stood there watching him weep.

"I love her. I love her so much. I know I screwed up. But I still love her. And I miss her. It just won't stop hurting."

Gerald just stood there for a few minutes waiting for Kyle to finish crying his eyes out. Then Gerald lifted Kyle up and carried him back to the car. After dropping Kyle off at Fred's place Gerald went back home to Anjelica. The moment he walked in the door she had a laundry list of questions.

"Where have you been? I haven't seen you all day. You didn't leave a note. You won't answer your phone. For all I know you could be dead in a ditch somewhere."

"Sorry mom. Didn't know you'd miss me so much."

"Of course I'd miss you. This is the most time we've spent apart since we started dating.

"We've gone months on end without speaking before."

"We weren't boyfriend and girlfriend back then. We weren't living together and sleeping in the same bed. The rules are different now. You can't run off without telling me where you're going or how to find you."

"OK. I'm sorry."

Gerald hugged her and kissed her forehead.

"So where the hell were you all day? And why weren't you answering your phone?"

Gerald pulled out his phone and handed it to Anjelica.

"It's off."

"OK. But why?"

"Because I spent the day with Kyle."

Anjelica would've been shocked if she wasn't so confused.

"Kyle? My Kyle?"

Gerald nodded his head. Anjelica looked around the room, almost as if she was searching for the words to say.

"Why?"

Gerald rubbed the back of his neck.

"You said you were worried. That you couldn't get any answers. So I figured I'd check on him for you."

Anjelica was shocked at how happy that made her. She actively fought to suppress a smile. She worried it might upset her boyfriend a little if she was too happy to hear about her ex.

"Oh. How is he?"

Gerald looked into her eyes. He didn't want to see any more sadness. He worried she might feel guilty if she knew how horribly Kyle was really doing…so Gerald lied.

"He's doing great. We spent the whole day at a fair."

Wow. Gerald wasn't expecting that. Anjelica seemed disappointed to hear that Kyle was doing fine. She was sullen for the rest of the night. When bedtime arrived Anjelica tried to initiate intercourse but Gerald said he wasn't in the mood. He could tell her heart wasn't in it. He couldn't stand being with her knowing she was thinking about Kyle the whole time.

Gerald didn't sleep that night. He couldn't even close his eyes. Two hours passed. Then three. He spent the first half of the night staring at the ceiling and the second half watching Anjelica sleep. He was thinking that if he didn't love her enough to do the right thing then he didn't deserve to be with her. When Anjelica woke up the next morning Gerald was sitting at the foot of the bed.

"Good morning."

"Mornin."

She yawned and stretched then rubbed her eyes.

"How long you been awake?"

"I never went to sleep."

Gerald never once turned to face her.

"What's wrong?"

Gerald closed his eyes, squeezing the lids tight trying to hold back tears. A few still fell.

"I'm breaking up with you."

Anjelica chortled.

"Yeah right. Come on."

Gerald didn't say a word. Never turned his head. Just silently stared at the wall. Anjelica was confused. Then worried. She jumped to her feet and ran to the other side of the bed. When she saw is tear-stained face her own eyes started watering.

"Why?"

Gerald turned away from her.

"Because you're still in love with Kyle."

Anjelica took a step back

"Why would you say that?"

"Because it's February. Valentine's Day is coming up. We should be celebrating our love. But you can't stop thinking about him."

"I'm worried about him. Just cause we're not together doesn't mean I stop caring."

Gerald rose to his feet. He'd been taller than her since high school but now he towered over her. He was always an imposing figure but that was the first time she'd ever felt real fear when looking at him.

"It's more than just concern. You were disappointed when I told you Kyle was doing great. It's cause you miss him and you're miserable without him. The only reason you aren't moping as much as him is cause you distracted yourself by jumping in bed with me."

Anjelica clutched her chest.

"Kyle's moping? You said he was fine?"

"I lied. His life's a mess. He's falling apart without you. And you just proved my point. Out of everything I said the only part you heard was Kyle, Kyle, Kyle. And you actually seem relieved to hear he's not doing well."

"Relieved? You think I'm happy to hear he's not doing well?"

"I think you're happy to know he still loves you."

Anjelica fell silent. She couldn't defend herself anymore. Everything Gerald said was right.

"Let's go."

Gerald held out his hand.

"Go where?"

"To see Kyle."

Anjelica paused for a moment before taking Gerald's hand. Gerald led her to the car and he jumped in the driver's seat. They drove to Fred's place in silence.

"Wait here."

Anjelica stayed in the car while Gerald headed inside. Fred said Kyle hadn't moved from the spot where Gerald dropped him. Gerald sat down on top of Kyle. Kyle groaned but made no effort to move Gerald.

"Wakey wakey."

"We're not going back to the fair."

"No, but you are getting out of this bed and walking out the door.

"You can't just bully me into being happy."

"Sorry Kyle, but tough love is the only kind I know. So unless your other friends are gonna do something to stop you from self-destructing I'm what you're stuck with."

"I have every right to be miserable."

"No, you don't. Not right now."

"Why can't you just leave me alone? Can't you see I'm in pain?"

"Yeah. I can. That's why I'm doing this."

Gerald yanked the covers of the bed and poured a water bottle over Kyle's head. Kyle jumped to his feet ready to throw punches.

"What the hell is wrong with you?"

"I'm trying to fix this."

"There's nothing left to fix! You said she found someone new! I have nothing left to live for!"

"You have everything to live for!"

"All I have left is heartache and suffering!"

"That's exactly what life is! Life is pain. Life is heartache. Life is suffering. Life is endless hours of anger and sadness. Life is relentless anguish. Life is memories that never stop hurting no matter how deep you bury them. There's no escaping the torment.

But every now and then you get a break. A few seconds a day when you can escape from life. And that's the hard part. Taking those few moments here and there and trying your dam best to make life worth it."

"How can losing Anje possibly be worth it?"

"You haven't lost her yet. She's outside waiting for you."

Kyle's eyes went wide with shock, fear, excitement and amazement. He was paralyzed.

"Life kicked you in the ass. You have every right to feel down. But I'm asking you, as a friend, get off your ass and go talk to her."

Anjelica was sitting in the car, fidgeting. Gerald took the keys so she couldn't change her mind and leave, so she had no radio to listen to. He dragged her out of bed so quickly se didn't think to grab her phone or tablet. All she could do was squirm around in her seat.

She was getting anxious. Feeling tired of waiting she jumped out of the car and started pacing around. The front door opened. Anjelica panicked. She leaned against the car door, trying her best to look aloof. She crossed her arms, uncrossed them to fix her hair, then crossed them again.

When Gerald stepped out the door she couldn't believe how nervous she got. Especially when she saw the look on his face. He seemed defeated. Her head was swimming. Maybe Kyle didn't want to see her. Did she make a mistake? Was she wrong to wait this long? Maybe she never should've dumped him in the first place.

Gerald walked over, stopping a foot in front of Anjelica. He stared at her, not saying a word. She couldn't bring herself to say anything either. She wanted to know what was wrong but feared the answer so much that she couldn't bring her lips to move. Then, Gerald stepped to the side and Anjelica could see Kyle standing in the doorway.

His hair was a mess. He had a patchy beard. She could literally see the stink lines rising from his shoulders. (Yes, I just used literally figuratively. Sue me!) Still…it felt so dam good to see him. She started walking forward. Kyle did as well. They stood in the middle of the lawn, awkwardly staring at each other.

"Hi."

"Hi."

After a few seconds of silence Gerald jumped in the front seat of the car.

"I'll leave you two alone."

They didn't respond. They didn't even hear him. They were so wrapped up in each other that his voice never reached their ears. As Gerald drove away he peeked in the rearview. Anjelica followed Kyle inside. Gerald took his foot off the gas, letting the car roll to a stop and putting on the parking brake. Then he put his head on the steering wheel and started crying.

No one heard from Gerald for the rest of the month. He refused to answer any phone calls, never went online. He found a coworker who let him crash on the couch for a few weeks and avoided all the usual places people would think to look for him. He even skipped a few classes in case Anjelica decided to wait outside the door for him.

Of course, even a perfect plan has flaws. Gerald was only human after all. One day he was feeling stressed and decided to visit his favorite park so he could lie in the grass staring at clouds. There weren't many in the sky. A few wisp here and there. Then, the blaring sun was suddenly interrupted, blocked out by Anjelica's smiling face hovering upside down above him.

"Hey."

"Hey."

Anjelica leaned forward and gave Gerald a gentle peck on the forehead.

"You are the most wonderful human on the face of the earth."

"I'm guessin' you and Kyle got back together."

"I love you Gerald. I really do. I'm sorry I can't love you the way you want me to."

"Don't worry 'bout it."

Gerald sat upright, brushing some grass off his head and shoulders.

"Imagine how easy life would be if we had any control over who we fell in love with."

"If that's how things worked, I'd definitely choose you."

If Gerald were a more sarcastic person he might've said something along the lines of "well that makes everything better. All my problems in life have just been solved." He barely mustered the strength to say "I know." He rose to his feet and turned to face Anjelica, who was squatting down in front of him. He held out his hand. She grabbed it and pulled herself up.

"I'm the luckiest girl in the world to have a friend as amazing as you. I promise to never forget that."

Gerald's heart sank. His face dropped and he lowered his eyes to the ground as he slowly pulled his hands away from hers.

"Maybe it would be better if you did."

Anjelica scrunched her face.

"What's that supposed to mean?"

Gerald closed his eyes and turned his head to the side. Anjelica stated feeling scared.

"Gerald….don't…"

Gerald look back at Anjelica with watery eyes.

"I don't think we can be friends anymore."

Anjelica started tearing up.

"Why?"

"I've been in love with you for as long as I can remember. I tried to ignore it. I tried to move on. But all these years later, after all the tears I cried, I still can't figure a way to get you outta my heart."

Teardrops fell from Anjelica's eyes. She brushed loose strands of hair off her face.

"But why does that mean we can't be friends? Is it cause we dated? Is it too weird now? I'm sorry Gerald. I take it all back. Let's forget we ever hooked up."

Gerald shook his head.

"I'm sorry Anje. It just hurts too much to be around you right now. The only way for me to stop loving you is with time and space."

Anjelica was full on bawling. Her legs were quivering. Gerald was stubbornly keeping his face stone but plenty of tears rolled down his cheeks.

"I don't want you to not be in my life. You've been such a great friend to me all these years."

Gerald sniffled and rubbed his nose.

"No I haven't. All that time, everything I did was for me. I've been so selfish. I always wanted to be the one to make you smile. I always hated seeing you smile when it had nothing to do with me. Between the two of us, you've always been the better friend. I'm the lucky one."

Anjelica was crying so much she could hardly get the words out.

"If this is what you need to do I won't stop you, but…I'll miss you."

Gerald swallowed a lump in his throat.

"I love you Anje. I will always love you."

He turned around and walked away, tears falling like waterfalls. He never once turned back to look at her. He didn't have to. He could hear her wailing. He wanted to comfort her. He couldn't. He knew that if he turned around right now he wouldn't be able to stop himself from running back to her. It was the hardest choice he ever made in his life…but it was the right one. It hurt like hell.

Just Shy of Serenity

Chapter 11

Two Years Later

Anjelica felt something was weird the moment she stirred from her sleep. As she stretched out she reached over and felt an empty space where Kyle would normally be. As she groggily meandered out of the bedroom the smell of hot coffee wafted into her nose. She closed her eyes and inhaled deeply. When she opened them Kyle was handing her a steaming hot cup.

"I figured this would get you out of bed."

When Kyle handed her the cup Anjelica realized it wasn't glass or porcelain in her hands. She looked down and saw she was holding a steel thermos. Across the room a fully dressed Kyle was slipping on some sneakers.

"Where you goin?"

"We."

He walked over to her with a long black cloth in his hand.

"What's that?"

"It's a blindfold."

"We ain't doing anythin' kinky this early in the mornin'." Kyle chuckled.

"Get dressed and meet me in the car. You don't have to put the blindfold on til we start drivin'. And don't worry 'bout makeup. We're not goin' anywhere public."

Kyle sat in the car waiting for what felt like forever for a disheveled Anjelica to stumble into the passenger seat.

"What's all this about?"

Kyle wrapped the cloth around Anjelica's eyes. He didn't tie it very tight. Just enough to stay in place.

"Where are we going?"

"Stop asking so many questions. Just relax. Go back to sleep."

Anjelica laughed off the suggestion only to then follow it. With her eyes covered and only the sound of the radio she quickly drifted off. Next thing she knew Kyle was shaking her. She reached up to remove the blindfold but Kyle reached out to grab her hands.

"Give me one second."

Kyle let go of her hands. Anjelica felt the car swaying then heard a door slam.

"Kyle? Kyle?"

Anjelica heard her door open. A hand touched hers, hopefully Kyle's. She felt a tug and reached her feet out. She touched solid ground and took steps forward. She kept moving her feet, following the tug, hoping she wasn't being kidnapped by some drug dealer for ransom. Kyle doesn't have a hidden past right?

They stopped moving. Kyle stepped behind Anjelica and took the blindfold off. She was staring at a one story building that looked like it should be condemned. Holes in every wall. Half the roof missing. Paint peeling. Her jaw dropped like an anvil. Kyle stepped in front of her with wide arms and an even wider smile.

"So…whadda ya think?"

"What is it?"

"Ours."

"Ours?"

"I bought it."

"You bought it? This piece of shit? Why?"

"Mostly because a shitty run down house is all I can afford on my own."

"Why not get a loan? Or borrow from your parents? Or ask me to pitch in?"

"This was supposed to be a present for you. Not much of a surprise if you know about it."

Kyle walked back towards the car while Anjelica continued to strain her eyes at the horrendous structure, struggling to envision the thought process that led to Kyle's decision.

"But…why?"

Anjelica spun around and Kyle was down on one knee pulling a small black box out of his pocket. Anjelica gasped as she took steps back and covered her face with her hands.

"Oh my god."

Kyle opened the box and held it up. The sunlight reflected on the diamond's smooth cuts. Anjelica's eyes watered.

"The plumbing needs to be completely redone. The roof is collapsing. For all intents and purposes I basically bought a plot of land and we're gonna have to build a house from scratch. But if we take our time together, build it brick by brick, when it's done we can set a wedding date and move all our stuff in."

"That's a lot of work. Not to mention with the money you spend on materials, workers and inspections. Why not just buy a new one."

"I did crunch the numbers baby and this one's surprisingly cheaper. Only a down payment so I own it outright. We're paying for materials either way but we save the most money by doing as much of our own labor as we can. Over the years maintenance and upkeep might add up, but, you can't guarantee that one way or the other.

"You really thought everything through huh?"

"For the past two years every time I looked at you I couldn't stop thinking...I never wanna go a single day without seeing your face."

Tears were rolling down Anjelica's cheeks.

"So...whadda ya say? You wanna build a life, a house, and a family with me?"

Anjelica paused for a few seconds to stare at him. Then she leapt into his arms.

"Of course I will."

For the next year Anjelica and Kyle spent every free second they had, every weekend and holiday, tearing that place down, rebuilding the walls and ceilings, toiling over garbage dumps for usable spare parts to save money wherever they could. Slowly, it started looking like an actual house. Humberto and members of Kyle's family would help from time to time. Thank god Kyle's brother is an electrician. That alone saved them a ton of money and hassle.

Once the major construction was done, everything had been inspected and cleared, the only thing left to do was set a date for the wedding. Two weeks before the wedding, the house fully painted and furnished, the lease was up on Anjelica and Kyle's apartment. It didn't make sense to sign a new one for such a short period but they were both set on not moving into the new house till they were married. Kyle wanted to carry his wife across the threshold.

After discussing it, Anjelica and Kyle moved the majority of their things into the house, saving a few bags of clothes and other essentials to take with them. Kyle paid for another month and stayed in the apartment while Anjelica moved in with her father. The moment she walked in the front door she dropped her suitcase, backpack and jaw. There, seated on the couch next to her father, wearing a dark blue polo shirt, his pants ironed and pressed, was Gerald.

"Hey."

"Hey."

Gerald rose to his feet, staring at Anjelica with a wide smile. She ran over and leapt into his arms, her heart overflowing with emotions. She was on the verge of tears.

"It's so good to see you. How long has it been?"

"Three years, 3 months and 6 days. But who's counting?"

Anjelica pulled back and cupped Gerald's face in her hands.

"You look so different. Your face is so smooth. Do you moisturize? And what's with these clothes? Are you modeling or something?"

"I've been told I clean up well. You don't look half bad yourself."

"Oh please. I've got no makeup on and I'm basically wearing pajamas. I'm a mess right now."

"You always look amazing to me Anje."

She threw her arms around his neck and gave him a big squeeze.

"I've missed you."

"I've missed you too."

"Where have you been all this time? And why are you showing up now?"

"I heard you were getting married."

Anjelica was cautiously optimistic. She hadn't seen Gerald in years yet right now things felt exactly the same. Like he was never gone. If nothing had changed she couldn't help but wonder the exact reason why he came. Gerald grabbed Anjelica by the hand and led her up the stairs.

"So, are you a doctor yet?"

"Nearly. I'm finishing med school and about to start my internship. How 'bout you?"

"I got my masters. Spent the last couple years volunteering."

"Are you a social worker now?"

"Almost. I officially received my license but decided to take some time off before starting."

"Why?"

They stopped in front of Anjelica's room. The door was closed.

"Truth is, I've been here a while."

"What do you mean?"

"Well, I heard you were staying with your dad for a couple weeks. I wanted to do something special. My wedding present to you, is right behind this door."

Her eyes went wide.

"Is it big?"

"It's huge. And expensive."

Anjelica smiled and reached for the door. Gerald reached out and grabbed her hands before she could turn the knob.

"Before you open it, there's a bit of an explanation."

Anjelica bit her lower lip.

"Do you remember the day we met?"

Anjelica giggled.

"Of course I do. You were coloring a zebra orange. I told you it was wrong."

"Actually, the zebra was purple. The lake was orange."

"I'm pretty sure the zebra was orange."

Gerald reached into his pocket and pulled out a folded up paper. He handed it to Anjelica and she unfolded it, revealing a purple zebra, orange lake, green sky, yellow grass and blue tree with grey leaves.

"Why do you have this?"

"It's very important to me. Because of this picture I made my very first friend."

Anjelica threw her arms around Gerald and squeezed him tight. He was trying to hide his joy but Anjelica could feel it very clearly.

"You're in a hugging mood today."

"I've got three years to make up for."

Gerald wrapped his arms around her, holding her tight. He felt himself enveloped in her smell. He could stay lost in that moment till the end of time.

"Do you remember that same year, we were talking about our dreams? You said you wanted to live under the sea."

"Yeah. After watching The Little Mermaid. I decided I wanted to live in the ocean."

Gerald pushed Anjelica back so he could look in her eyes.

"Well, I still haven't figured out a way for humans to breathe under water…So I figured we could bring the ocean to us."

Gerald reached for the doorknob, turned it and pushed the door open. He stepped aside and motioned Anjelica forward. She stepped past him and her heart stopped. Everything was blue. The carpet, the ceiling, the dresser, nightstand and even the door. Her bed was covered in ocean bedsheets and a comforter with fish swimming through the water. The walls were lined with matching ocean wallpaper.

There were stuffed animals everywhere. A shark hung from the ceiling by strings. An octopus carefully draped over the corner of the dresser. Dolphins, stingrays, sea turtles and a variety of fish were placed in every corner of the room. On the bed was a blue whale so large that even with its nose touching the headboard the tail was hanging over the foot of the bed.

"It's a wedding tradition right? Something old, your bedroom, something new, the decorations, something blue, well...we might've gone a little overboard there."

Anjelica was speechless. Tears were raining down from each eye. Gerald pointed to the picture in her hand.

"And you can borrow that until the wedding is over."

Anjelica once again jumped into Gerald's arms.

"Thank you Gerald. For everything."

The day of the wedding Gerald was one of the first people to show up at the church. He wanted to make sure he got a seat in the very front so Anjelica could see his smiling face. She noticed him, and was grateful to see him there, but obviously she barely paid attention to him. She spent the majority of the event staring at Kyle.

Since Gerald didn't rsvp it was hard finding a place for him to sit at the reception. He ended up tucked away in a dark corner of the room with all the other misfits. The exact place he would've naturally migrated to had there been no assigned seating. Once the guest had all settled in, and the food had been served, Kyle's brother stood up to deliver his speech.

"I don't believe in soul mates, but I do believe in math. While it's true that there are plenty of fish in the sea, how many of those fish are right for you? How many of them are an appropriate age? Have the same taste in food and music?

Of the billions of people on this planet…how many of them are we actually compatible with?

Then you have to take into account random chance. What if you meet the right person, but it's not the right time? You're not in the right place in your life? Or maybe they're not in the right place in theirs? There's a distance between you, be it physical or emotional, and you two never quite come together.

What I'm trying to say is, it's entirely possible that there might only be three to five people that, not only are they capable of loving us as much as we love them, but we're actually capable of having a long lasting relationship with. So when you find someone you have a deep connection with…you gotta do everything you can to preserve it.

Kyle, Anje, marriage is a rollercoaster. Lots of ups and down, twist and turns. The only way to make it to the end is to get there together. So grab onto each other's hands and hold on tight. You're in for the ride of your lives. Cheers."

The entire room shouted "cheers!" and raised their glasses. Gerald was staring at Anjelica with a smile on his face and tears in his eyes. Anyone who saw him would assume he was crying because of the happy occasion. He wished that were true. Anjelica looked in his direction and they locked eyes. She smiled and waved. It felt like a knife in his heart.

For most of the night Gerald stayed in his seat, nursing some sort of peach flavored cocktail, watching Anjelica dance. The father daughter dance. The first dance as husband and wife. The Macarena. Once he was sure

Two Years Later

Anjelica was too distracted to notice he was missing Gerald slipped out the front door. As he was walking away he heard her voice.

"Gerald!"

Gerald turned around to see Anjelica running towards him, holding up the front of her dress so she didn't trip over it. Gerald had expected a girl would wear heels at her wedding. Anjelica had on white sneakers with pink glitter stripes.

"You're wearing sneakers at your wedding?"

"I never learned how to walk in heels. Plus, I was planning to dance all night."

"Of course you were."

Anjelica balled up a fist and punched Gerald in the arm.

"Ow. What was that for?"

"You were actually gonna sneak away without saying goodbye? Fuck you asshole!"

She punched him again.

"Sorry. I didn't think you'd notice."

"Of course I noticed. You haven't danced with me yet."

"I've never liked dancing."

"You've always danced with me before."

"I was trying to get in your pants back then."

Anjelica playfully shoved Gerald.

"I appreciate your honesty."

They laughed with each other, then silently stared in each other's eyes for a few seconds.

"Gerald...can I ask you a question?"

Gerald wanted to say no. He knew what she wanted to ask. He didn't want to tell her the truth. He knew she wouldn't believe the lie.

"Sure."

Anjelica moved a loose strand of hair from her face and placed it behind her ear.

"Are you still in love with me?"

Gerald scratched the back of his head and turned his head away.

"Is it that obvious?"

Anjelica chuckled.

"Gerald…you keep doing all these amazing things for me. Then you say it's just what friends do for each other. But it's not Gerald. You wouldn't break into Juan's house to redecorate his bedroom."

"Juan's boyfriend is an interior decorator. If I tried to redo their room they'd both kill me."

"I get that. The one thing I don't get is…why?"

"Why would Juan and his boyfriend kill me?"

"No. I mean…why are you in love with me?"

"Why are you in love with Kyle?"

"How could I not fall in love with him? He's cute, funny, sweet, smart. I don't, I just…I look at him and… I just feel love."

Gerald took steps forward until his forehead touched hers.

"That's the same way I feel about you."

Anjelica reached up to place a hand on Gerald's cheek.

"I'm sorry I couldn't love you back."

Gerald grabbed her hand.

"I forgive you. I know you would if you could."

He lowered her hand and tried to step away but Anjelica squeezed his hand tight.

"There's just one thing I want to ask you. Something that's been bugging me for years. I was scared to bring it up because it's a sensitive subject."

"Well, now's as good a time as any."

"In high school, when you ran away, I was so shocked. I never knew you were struggling so much. You never once told me anything was wrong. You hardly ever complained about anything."

"Is there a question in there somewhere?"

"How come you never reached out to me? How come you never asked for my help or support? Matter of fact, when I did try to help you pushed me away."

Gerald pulled his hand away from hers.

"I spent most of my childhood drowning in sorrow. I was scared to say anything to you because I didn't wanna drag you down with me."

"I'd gladly let you drag me down Gerald. You're my friend. I care about you so much. I wanted to help. I would've been there for you."

"I know. That's why I couldn't say anything. Because I love you. I can't stand the thought of doing something to make you cry."

"If that's true then you have to stay in my life. I need you Gerald. I can't stand the thought of never talking to you again. I know that being around me might be painful for you at times. I don't want to hurt you. That's the last thing I'd ever want. But never seeing you again would be way too painful for me. There's gotta be something in the middle."

Gerald was silent. He had no words to express what he felt. He was having trouble separating all the conflicting emotions.

"You don't have to call me every day. Just...promise you'll stay in touch. Please?"

Gerald placed a hand on the top of her head.

"I'll try my best."

She threw her arms around Gerald's waist and squeezed him tight. He gently wrapped his arms around her shoulders. Then she stepped back, grabbed his shoulders and pulled herself up to kiss his cheek.

"You should get back inside. You're husband probly misses you."

She looked in his eyes and a wave of sadness washed over her.

"I'm never gonna see you again am I?"

With her head hung low and her face dropping Anjelica turned around and started walking back to the reception.

"Hey Anje."

She spun around.

"Yeah?"

"Call me when you get back from your honeymoon. We can hang out."

Anjelica smiled.

"Ok. It's a date."

Anjelica ran back inside. Gerald turned around and walked away with a smile on his face. They both lived happily ever after. No, seriously, I mean it this time. Anjelica and Kyle would spend the rest of their lives together, raising three beautiful kids...but who cares? This isn't their story. This story was always about Gerald.

I'm choosing to end the story here because of what happened to Gerald in that moment. Part of him knew that he might never see Anjelica again. She tended to lean on him most when she was upset, drifting away when life was going well. A small part of Gerald hoped he'd never hear from her again. That would mean her life was going great.

As Gerald walked away his mind raced, retracing every step of his life, sorting through every memory he had of Anjelica. All the things they went through together, everything they went through separately. He wasn't sure if it was possible to ever stop loving her. It might never stop hurting that she didn't love him back.

Then he thought about how Anjelica was smiling all day. In that moment a thought entered Gerald's head. If he could relive his entire life over again...he wouldn't change a single thing. He wouldn't want to do anything that could risk wiping that smile off Anjelica's face. Actually...there's one thing he would change. Trust me, it's not what you think.

Just Shy of Serenity

Other Books by Nathan Lyle Cunningham

Series #1 | TOXIC – *Before the Beginning*

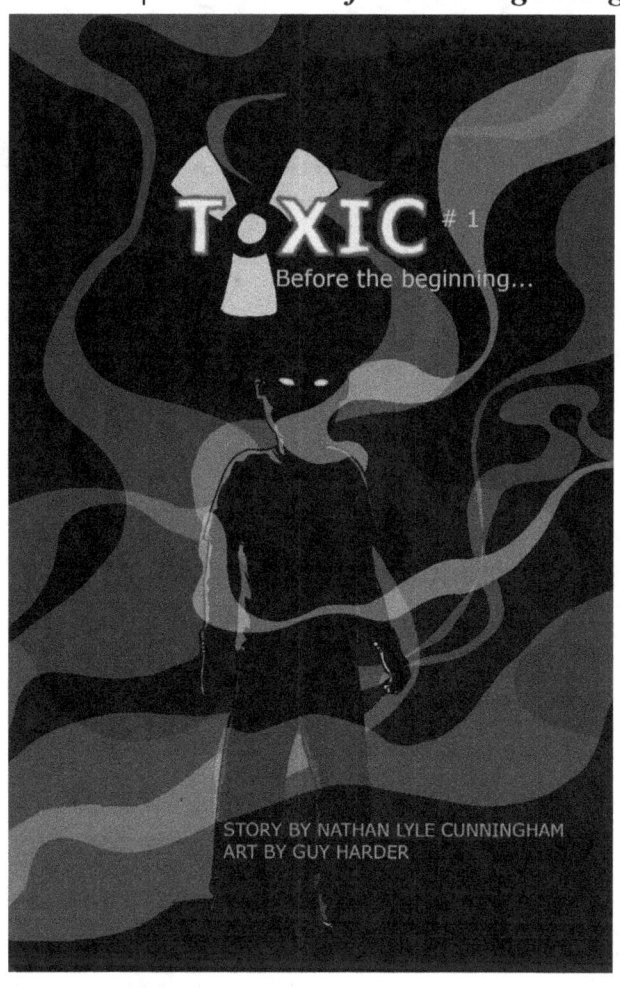

Series #2 | TOXIC

COMIC BOOK SERIES about Oscar Mireles, a boy from a town that was overrun with radiation. While more than half the town died somehow Oscar was infused with radiation. An accident that took many lives gave Oscar the power to save some. It gave him a great power, but it's also a great curse.

Everything Is Impossible

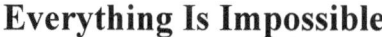

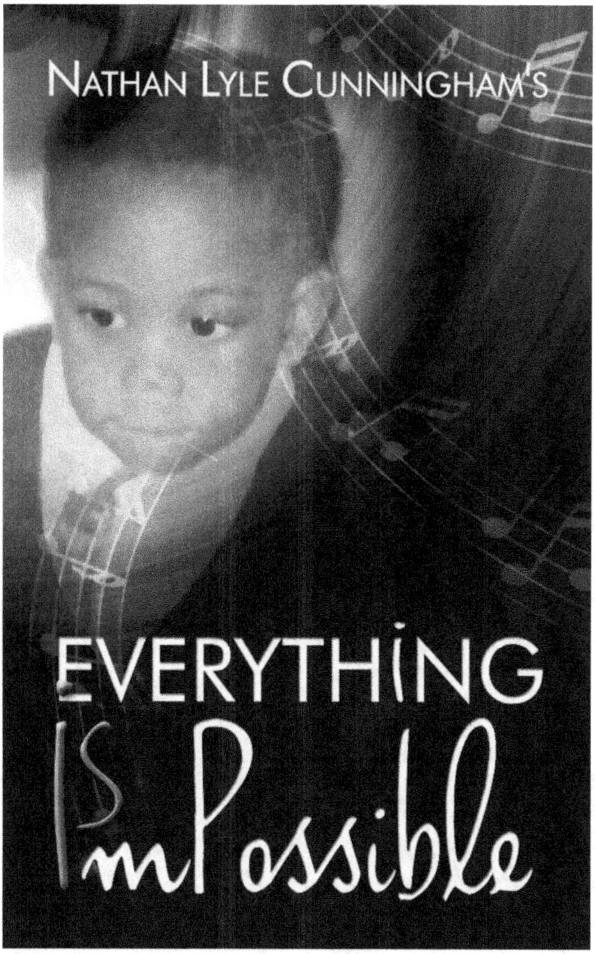
NATHAN LYLE CUNNINGHAM'S
EVERYTHING
IS
IMPOSSIBLE

I was physically abused at home. I was picked on and beaten up at school. I tried to kill myself every year of high school. I ran away as a teenager. I was homeless for two years. Somewhere in the middle of all this I found a dream worth chasing. This is the story of my life in my own words.

Forever. Amen

In *Forever. Amen.* five friends take turns detailing the most painful months of their lives: when a dear friend is diagnosed with cancer and they struggle to come to terms with her impending death.

The Marina

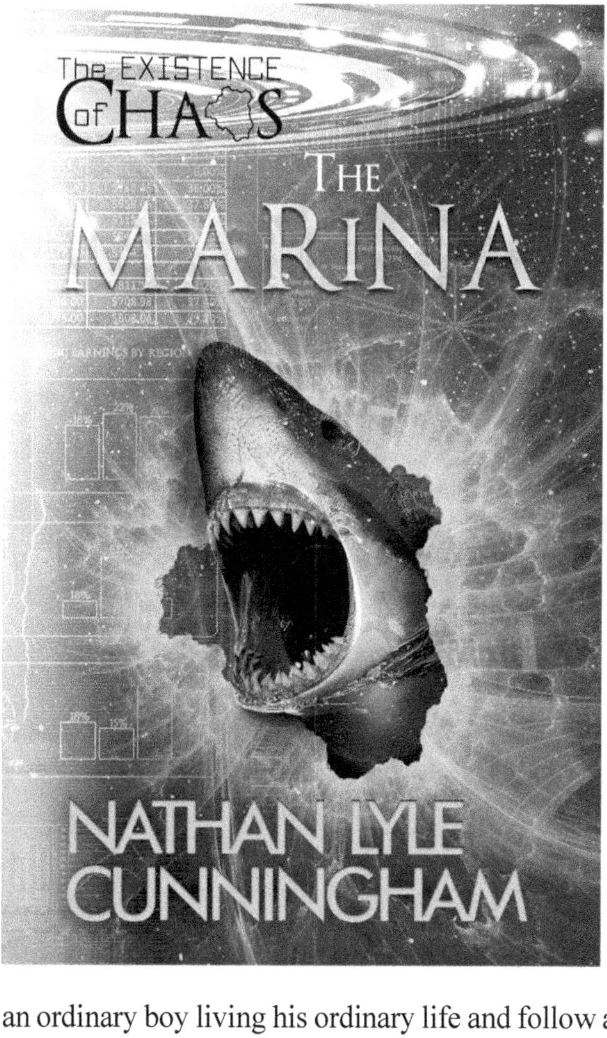

Meet an ordinary boy living his ordinary life and follow along as he beings an adventure beyond his wildest dreams.

Just Shy of Serenity

Other Books by Nathan Lyle Cunningham

Nathan Lyle Cunningham
www.YouTube.com/NathanLyleOfficial
www.Twitter.com/NathanLyle

www.ingramcontent.com/pod-product-compliance
Lightning Source LLC
Chambersburg PA
CBHW072001070526
44583CB00015B/1278